Family
Therapy

Theories of Psychotherapy Series

Cognitive–Behavioral Therapy
  Michelle G. Craske

Existential–Humanistic Therapy
  Kirk J. Schneider and Orah T. Krug

Family Therapy
  William J. Doherty and Susan H. McDaniel

Feminist Therapy
  Laura S. Brown

Relational–Cultural Therapy
  Judith V. Jordan

Theories of Psychotherapy Series
Jon Carlson and Matt Englar-Carlson, Series Editors

Family Therapy

William J. Doherty and Susan H. McDaniel

American Psychological Association

Washington, DC

Published by
American Psychological Association
750 First Street, NE
Washington, DC 20002
www.apa.org

To order
APA Order Department
P.O. Box 92984
Washington, DC 20090-2984
Tel: (800) 374-2721;
Direct: (202) 336-5510
Fax: (202) 336-5502;
TDD/TTY: (202) 336-6123
Online: www.apa.org/books/
E-mail: order@apa.org

In the U.K., Europe, Africa, and the Middle East, copies may be ordered from
American Psychological Association
3 Henrietta Street
Covent Garden, London
WC2E 8LU England

Typeset in Minion by Shepherd Inc., Dubuque, IA

Printer: Edwards Brothers, Ann Arbor, MI
Cover Designer: Minker Design, Sarasota, FL
Cover Art: *Lily Rising*, 2005, oil and mixed media on panel in craquelure frame, by Betsy Bauer.

The opinions and statements published are the responsibility of the authors, and such opinions and statements do not necessarily represent the policies of the American Psychological Association.

Library of Congress Cataloging-in-Publication Data

Doherty, William J. (William Joseph), 1945-
  Family therapy / William J. Doherty and Susan H. McDaniel.
    p. cm.
  Includes bibliographical references and index.
  ISBN-13: 978-1-4338-0549-3
  ISBN-10: 1-4338-0549-9
  1. Family psychotherapy. I. McDaniel, Susan H. II. American Psychological Association. III. Title.
  RC488.5.D628 2010
  616.89'156--dc22
                                2009018746

British Library Cataloguing-in-Publication Data
A CIP record is available from the British Library.

Printed in the United States of America
First Edition

To our students—of all disciplines

Contents

Series Preface

Some might argue that in the contemporary clinical practice of psychotherapy, evidence-based intervention and effective outcome have overshadowed theory in importance. Maybe. But, as editors of this series, we don't propose to take up that controversy here. We do know that psychotherapists adopt and practice according to one theory or another because their experience, and decades of good evidence, suggests that having a sound theory of psychotherapy leads to greater therapeutic success. Still, the role of theory in the helping process can be hard to explain. This narrative about solving problems helps convey theory's importance:

> Aesop tells the fable of the sun and wind having a contest to decide who was the most powerful. From above the earth, they spotted a man walking down the street, and the wind said that he bet he could get his coat off. The sun agreed to the contest. The wind blew and the man held on tightly to his coat. The more the wind blew, the tighter he held. The sun said it was his turn. He put all of his energy into creating warm sunshine and soon the man took off his coat.

What does a competition between the sun and the wind to remove a man's coat have to do with theories of psychotherapy? We think this deceptively simple story highlights the importance of theory as the precursor to any effective intervention—and hence to a favorable outcome. Without a guiding theory, we might treat the symptom without understanding the role of the individual. Or we might create power conflicts with our clients and not understand that, at times, indirect means of helping (sunshine) are often as effective—if not more so—than direct ones (wind). In the absence of theory, we might lose track of the treatment focus and instead get caught up in, for example, social correctness and not wanting to do something that looks too simple.

What exactly *is* theory? The *APA Dictionary of Psychology* defines theory as "a principle or body of interrelated principles that purports to explain or predict a number of interrelated phenomena." In psychotherapy, a theory is a set of principles used to explain human thought and behavior, including what causes people to change. In practice, a theory creates the goals of therapy and specifies how to pursue them. Haley (1997) noted that a theory of psychotherapy ought to be simple enough for the average therapist to understand but comprehensive enough to account for a wide range of eventualities. Furthermore, a theory guides action toward successful outcomes while generating hope in both the therapist and client that recovery is possible.

Theory is the compass that allows psychotherapists to navigate the vast territory of clinical practice. In the same ways that navigational tools have been modified to adapt to advances in thinking and ever-expanding territories to explore, theories of psychotherapy have changed over time. The different schools of theories are commonly referred to as *waves*, the first wave being psychodynamic theories (i.e., Adlerian, psychoanalytic), the second wave learning theories (i.e., behavioral, cognitive–behavioral), the third wave humanistic theories (person-centered, gestalt, existential), the fourth wave feminist and multicultural theories, and the fifth wave postmodern and constructivist theories. In many ways, these waves represent how psychotherapy has adapted and responded to changes in psychology, society, and epistemology as well as to changes in the nature of psychotherapy itself. Psychotherapy and the theories that guide it are dynamic and responsive. The wide variety of theories is also testament to the different ways in which the same human behavior can be conceptualized (Frew & Spiegler, 2008).

It is with these two concepts in mind—the central importance of theory and the natural evolution of theoretical thinking—that we developed the APA Theories of Psychotherapy Series. Both of us are thoroughly fascinated by theory and the range of complex ideas that drive each model. As university faculty members who teach courses on the theories of psychotherapy, we wanted to create learning materials that not only highlight the essence of the major theories for professionals and professionals in training but also clearly bring the reader up-to-date on the current status of the models. Often in books on theory, the biography of the original theorist overshadows the evolution of the model. In contrast, our intent was to highlight the contemporary uses of the theories as well as their history and context.

As this project began, we faced two immediate decisions: which theories to address and who best to present them. We looked at graduate-level theories of psychotherapy courses to see which theories are being taught, and we explored popular scholarly books, articles, and conferences to determine which theories draw the most interest. We then developed a dream list of authors from among the best minds in contemporary theoretical practice. Each author is one of the leading proponents of that approach as well as a knowledgeable practitioner. We asked each author to review the core constructs of the theory, bring the theory into the modern sphere of clinical practice by looking at it through a context of evidence-based practice, and clearly illustrate how the theory looks in action.

There are 24 titles planned for the series. Each title can stand alone or can be put together with a few other titles to create materials for a course in psychotherapy theories. This option allows instructors to create a course featuring the approaches they believe are the most salient today. To support this end, APA Books has also developed a DVD for each of the approaches that demonstrates the theory in practice with a real client. Some of the DVDs show therapy over six sessions. Contact APA Books for a complete list of available DVD programs (http://www.apa.org/videos).

In this book, Drs. Doherty and McDaniel clearly present family systems theory and practice. Because people do not exist alone, it is necessary to understand numerous social and cultural dynamics and how they affect individuals. This approach shows how to understand the context and systems dynamics that affect clients as well as how to change those that are harmful. Although the title of this monograph is "family therapy," the model also applies to working with individual clients. Drs. McDaniel and

Doherty draw upon their vast experience as practicing psychotherapists and researchers to provide a clear and concise description of family theory and practice.

—John Carlson and Matt Englar-Carlson

REFERENCES

Frew, J., & Spiegler, M. (2008). *Contemporary psychotherapies for a diverse world*. Boston: Lahaska Press.

Haley, J. (1997). *Leaving home: The therapy of disturbed young people*. New York: Routledge.

Family
Therapy

1

Introduction

Family therapy is a lot more than working with families on their inter-personal problems. It's a way of thinking in systemic, relational terms and a set of strategies for intervening with individuals, couples, families, and other systems. Contemporary family therapy is not defined by a head count of who is in the therapist's office; although family therapists usually prefer to have access to multiple family members, they can work with just one individual. Similarly, family therapists apply their systems approach by forging collaborative relationships between families and community organizations that serve families. The purview of treatment of family therapy is the whole gamut of psychological and relational problems treated by psychotherapists, plus other problems treated by teams of medical and psychological professionals.

For a formal definition of family therapy, we turn to one offered by a distinguished group of family therapy researchers assembled by the National Institute of Mental Health:

> Family therapy is a psychotherapeutic approach that focuses on alter-ing interactions between a couple, with a nuclear or extended family, or between a family and other interpersonal systems, with the goal of

alleviating problems initially presented by individual family members, family subsystems, the family as a whole, or other referral sources. (Wynne, 1988, p. 9)

Central to this definition is the focus on changing relationships and interactions as a way to treat human problems. This does not imply that relationship problems are the only or chief source of psychological problems; although some prominent pioneers in the field rejected psychiatric diagnosis and biological sources of mental illness, most contemporary family therapists accept the idea that problems can have biological, psychological, familial, sociological, cultural, and environmental sources. Nor does the emphasis on relationships and interactions imply that family therapists do not use models and tools of individual psychotherapy; it's just that they focus on healing people's relationships as a primary pathway to recovery.

Take the example of a mildly depressed, middle-aged adult working with a therapist on a complicated relationship with a now-frail parent. Therapists of all practice models would help the patient or client[1] understand the complexities of this life long relationship and the current resentment and ambivalence the patient feels about the parent. All therapists would help the patient manage his or her feelings and actions in a healthy manner. A family therapist would probably add the following elements to this work: (a) a nuanced exploration of how extended family of origin dynamics (current dynamics and not just past ones) are hurting the parent–child relationship and might interfere with the patient's efforts to change; (b) encouragement for the patient to work on healing the relationship now as a healthy move for the patient, the parent, and the rest of the family; and (c) an invitation to facilitate this healing by working directly with the patient and the parent and even other family members, if appropriate. A family therapist would also be thinking about the benefits for subsequent generations of healing this key family relationship before the death of the parent.

Although there are many family therapy models, the heart of all approaches is systems theory, which came out of mid-20th century

---

[1] Because much of our work has been in medical settings, we generally use the term "patient" rather than "client," although we acknowledge that many counselors and therapists prefer client.

biology, physics, chemistry, and cybernetics. The technical features of systems theory will be described in a later chapter, but for now we emphasize that this way of thinking transcends the reductionist bias in Western culture towards understanding phenomena by breaking them down to their smallest parts. In the realm of psychotherapy, it's the reductionist assumption is that psychological problems can be explained by understanding how individuals function (psychologically or biologically) without a complex understanding of their interpersonal environment. Don Jackson (1957) and other family therapy pioneers became frustrated after treating children successfully and then seeing them relapse when they returned home. They reached for theoretical understanding of how the intimate social environment affected what had been seen as entrenched individual disorders, and they came upon general systems theory and cybernetic theory as ways to understand how families worked.

A word about terminology: Although alternative terms such as family group psychotherapy and family systems therapy have occasionally been used in professional literature, we employ the term *family therapy* because it has been most widely used since the late 1950s. Similarly, because family therapy has always been multidisciplinary (including professionals who describe themselves as family psychologists, family psychiatrists, family counselors, family psychiatric nurses, clinical social workers, and marriage and family therapists), we mostly use the generic term *family therapist* because it includes all of these groups.

Making a systemic way of thinking understandable is a key goal for this book. Because systemic thinking has to be grasped intuitively and not just conceptually, we will move back and forth between concepts and illustrations. Even for readers who never see themselves as practicing family therapy in the future, understanding family systems dynamics can be crucial for success as an individual therapist. Family and intimate partners are always involved in patients' efforts to recover and change; the therapist is just one player, and usually the most recent one. When therapists see family members block recovery of their patient, a lack of a nuanced understanding of family systems leads some individually oriented therapists to judgmental family blaming that does not help the patient. Family therapists, on the other hand, tend to have a more compassionate understanding that families will do what they know how to do, will sometimes feel threatened by change, and will play out their accustomed roles without necessarily having ill will or psychopathology. A family therapist sees the whole family system, and beyond, as a focus of work in therapy, even if only an individual is the patient. It is this systems, ecological stance that uniquely informs the thinking and practice of family therapy.

This book also aims to teach the common elements across different models of family therapy and to give enough of a flavor of specific models to encourage follow-up learning. We seek to convey the dynamism and continual unfolding of family therapy as it has moved through different generations of approaches, has backed away from the rigidities of its founding decades, has become more evidence based, and has reached out to other healing systems and communities. Welcome aboard for this journey into the complex and practically useful world of family therapy.

History

Histories of psychotherapy models generally deal exclusively with the professional origins of each approach—theories, clinical insights, research evidence—while ignoring the social and cultural milieu out of which the model emerged. This is an unfortunate omission because every approach to therapy is shaped by its historical environment. We treat the ills our time with the tools that seem to fit the historical moment, as Freud did with psychoanalysis in late Victorian Europe (Gay, 2006). For this reason, we begin with broader historical and cultural developments in the United States during the era when family therapy was founded and then focus on the professional development of the field. We draw on Doherty and Baptiste (1993) for the first part of the discussion.

SOCIOCULTURAL BACKGROUND

Although family therapy was born in the 1950s, it was the culmination of influences initially visible in the 1920s and 1930s, a period of serious popular and professional concern for the well-being of American families (Howard, 1981). Divorce was increasing and multigenerational family solidarity was being eroded by industrialization and urbanization.

Child neglect became a significant concern for the society at large. During the earlier Progressive Era (1890–1920), social reform had been seen as the way to solve the social problems of families. But when the Progressive Era waned in the aftermath of World War I, American and European culture turned away from social reform to the personal dimension of life.

Americans in the 1950s were very family focused. There was strong concern over the integrity of the American family as an institution and an emphasis on returning to traditional gender roles in the aftermath of World War II. The strong American family was a seen as a bulwark against communism (Tyler-May, 1989). The culture of the 1950s celebrated close family bonds but was also ambivalent about them. Loyalty to family and social institutions was fostered, but cultural critics worried that individuality was being lost (Whyte's [1956] *The Organization Man* was a big best seller). Full-time mothering was lauded, but at the same time "overbearing mothers" were blamed for their children's behavioral problems, and psychologists worried about male role models for boys (Lamb, 2003). Family therapy was created to treat the "enmeshed," smothering family; most of the pioneers focused on ways to understand and intervene with overly tight family bonds causing problems for individuals. Every therapy model is shaped by the culture of its origin and is challenged to adapt to cultural change. We are now in a different era of family life, with greater concerns about the fraying of family bonds (Doherty, 1995). Part of the ongoing story of family therapy is just this kind of adaptation.

A final note about context: Along with behavioral therapy, family therapy was the first home-grown American form of psychotherapy. As such, it reflected Americans' pragmatic interest in action and problem solving as opposed to deep introspection and lengthy treatment. Americans saw themselves as rebuilding the world after World War II. Why not rebuild families as a way to treat emotional problems in an activist, optimistic fashion? To borrow a contemporary phrase, family therapy has always reflected the quintessential American spirit of "yes, we can."

Alongside the cultural roots of family therapy were the pioneering psychological theorists and psychotherapists of the first half of the 20th century. Freud introduced the radical notion that psychological disorders stemmed from unresolved childhood problems, which in turn were rooted in early family relationships. Adler, with his strong emphasis on "social embeddedness," added an emphasis on current family relationships and pioneered seeing family members together as an adjunct to other forms of treatment (Hoffman, 1994; Nichols, 2008). In the United States, Harry Stack Sullivan (1953) developed an interpersonal theory of psychiatry that influenced later family therapists. In England, John Bowlby (1949) began to see parents and children together in the 1940s, although always as an aid to individual therapy, which was considered the core treatment. None of these great figures took the next step to formulate a model of family therapy in which the family was emphasized on its own terms as the cornerstone of the treatment process (Nichols, 2008).

We organize the professional history of family therapy along the lines suggested by Hanna (2007) into three generations. The first generation was the radical founders who challenged the status quo, reached outside of the therapy world for new theories, and set the template for the family therapy field. The second generation was the challengers who questioned the assumptions of the founders, reached outside the field for inspiration, and developed their own models. Third were the integrators who developed specialized, evidence-based models for particular populations.

THE FIRST GENERATION

The first generation radical founders of family therapy included the Palo Alto Team, Murray Bowen, Salvador Minuchin, and the creators of strategic family therapy. These great thinkers and therapists minds created the groundwork on which this model developed. In this section we will give a few details about what they accomplished.

The Palo Alto Team

Among the earliest insights that led to family therapy was Gregory Bateson's (1958, 1972) anthropological work in 1935 and 1936. In his study of the Iatuml people in New Guinea, Bateson developed the idea of "schismogenesis," which he defined as "a process of differentiation in the norms of individual behavior resulting from cumulative interaction between individuals" (1958, p. 175). Bateson was interested in how people use social interaction to create stability and change in their relationships. Unlike psychological theories that focus on behavior as stemming from factors inside the individual and sociological theories that focus on the larger environmental influences, Bateson focused on the level of the "in between": how the dances people do together shape their behavior. He wrote: "We have got to consider, not only A's reaction to B's behavior, but we must go on to consider how these affect B's later behavior and the effect of this on A" (1958, p. 176). Indeed, he wished to define the discipline of social psychology as "the study of the reactions of individuals to the reactions of other individuals" (1958, p. 175). Once this area became a focus of interest, Bateson maintained, the fundamental question becomes how the relationship between these individuals changes over time by means of dynamics internal to the relationship. This idea may seem commonplace now, but it was revolutionary at the time.

Bateson defined complementary schismogenesis as occurring when two individuals' (or groups') behavior each invites the opposite response from the other (e.g., dominance and submission). He noted that this pattern can escalate progressively unless other factors are present to restrain the excesses of the two behavioral tendencies. The other kind of schismogenesis is symmetrical, in which the same kind of response is elicited between the individuals or groups (e.g., boasting begets boasting). Here too the pattern can become progressive and damaging if not restrained by dynamics internal to the relationship; in other words, people and groups of people develop mechanisms to get off whatever merry-go-round they are on together; otherwise, the relationship would implode or explode. With this writing in the mid-1930s, Bateson introduced the notion of circular interaction processes that was to become the cornerstone of family therapy theory. But Bateson was not satisfied that he had the right frame for his insights: Schismogenesis did not seem like a fertile enough conceptualization (Bateson, 1958).

During the World War II period, a time of waiting and holding on for social scientists all over the world, Bateson joined a small group of luminaries, including his wife Margaret Mead, as well as Ruth Benedict, Gardiner Murphy, and Erik Erikson, who clung together through regular visits to the farm of psychologist Lawrence Frank in New Hampshire

(Bateson, 1984). The informal think tank was also visited from time to time by Norbert Weiner, the mathematician/engineer who developed one of the principal intellectual and practical innovations of the century: cybernetics, the founding science of the computer age. In discussions with Bateson during the warm New Hampshire summers, Weiner provided the key that Bateson was looking for in his theory of social interaction: the focus on messages and communication rather than on objects or forces. Intrigued by how cybernetics could help explain the way circular interactions regulate behavior and perhaps motivated by his own experience in psychoanalysis, Bateson began to study therapist–patient interactions after the war.

Together with psychiatrist colleague Jurgen Reusch, Bateson developed a groundbreaking theory of levels of interpersonal communication: the verbal, or digital, and the nonverbal, or analogic (Reusch & Bateson, 1951). Applying Whitehead and Russell's theory of logical types, Bateson proposed that the analogic channel of communication provides the context for the digital. For example, the words may say "I care about you," and the tone or facial expression may say "I want you to do what I tell you to do." The contextual message is termed the *metamessage*; it classifies the verbal message by telling us how to interpret it. (This idea is now a cornerstone of the field of communication.) Always a naturalist like his geneticist father, Bateson analyzed these communication phenomena in the behavior of otters at the San Francisco zoo, as well as in therapist–patient encounters in clinics (Lipset, 1982).

In 1952, Bateson began assembling a young research team in Palo Alto, California, to study human and animal communication. Each member of the team later became a principal figure in family therapy: Jay Haley, John Weakland, Don Jackson, and later Paul Watzlawick and Virginia Satir. Starting with studies of dogs, films, hypnosis, and psychotherapy, this group later observed and studied the families of patients with schizophrenia. As a part of the progressive movement in the culture of the 1950s, this research group was visited and influenced by luminaries such as cybnerneticist Norbert Weiner and Alan Watts, the theologian of Eastern mysticism (Lipset, 1982).

In a classic paper that marked the birth of family systems theory, Bateson, Jackson, Haley, and Weakland (1956) provided the first detailed analysis of communication in families. The analysis focused on a phenomenon Bateson and his colleagues called the double bind, which they defined as a sequence of communication in which there was a contradiction between the contextual level and the verbal level. For example, a father gives his adolescent son an injunction, such as "Do not do this, or I will punish you," followed by a contradicting injunction, usually nonverbal, such as "If you obey me, I will not respect you because you're not acting like a man." Another example is the "be spontaneous" paradox, in which a spouse demands more affection and appreciation from the partner and then rejects it when offered because it is not authentic—"you're just saying that because I asked you to." The double bind here is that it is impossible to comply with a demand for a behavior that by definition is supposed to be freely given.

Having uncovered this subtle and destructive form of family communication, the Palo Alto team believed that schizophrenic symptoms would result from this pattern when it was enduring and intense and when the child was not free to comment on the contradiction. Although the team's own observational research with families in the late 1950s did not confirm the double-bind hypothesis for schizophrenia—double-bind communication was very hard to quantify and it seemed common in families without a member with mental illness—they had embarked on the unprecedented process of recording and analyzing family interactions. Bateson and his colleagues were particularly struck by the rigid patterns of interaction that families maintained over long periods of time. When one member attempted to change the pattern by trying new behavior, the family seemed to conspire to stop it. And yet, many of these families were quite close emotionally.

To understand how these families remained intact and stable despite many disruptions, Bateson turned to Weiner's cybernetic theory. Families, Bateson reasoned, were calibrated systems that, like a furnace, maintain themselves within tolerable limits. Bateson and his team proposed that dysfunctional families have rigid rules that in effect "require" the symptomatic member to remain in this role while the rest of the family maintains good appearances toward the outside world. Don Jackson (1957), in another classic article on the development of family therapy, offered the concept of "family homeostasis," which describes the tendency of all families to maintain habitual patterns of behavior. A family member's symptomatic behavior, then, can serve the internal logic of the family to maintain its stability. This idea helped Jackson to understand the apparently inexplicable tendency of some families to avoid meaningful change. In these families, there seemed to be a rule that someone must be emotionally troubled at any one time: If one child was "cured" by a therapist, another child or adult was likely to become ill, or a key relationship became stressed.

Subsequent to publishing the double-bind hypothesis paper in 1956, the Palo Alto team was pulled in the direction of clinical interventions, perhaps because their most visible contribution and most ready source of funding were in the area of understanding troubled families. Meeting with clinical families, however, made it increasingly difficult to separate observation from treatment. Jackson, Haley, and Weakland began experimenting with treating families dealing with schizophrenics in joint sessions. In 1959, this trend was formalized when Jackson became the first director of the Mental Research Institute in Palo Alto. This institute began to attract clinicians who were interested in the new modality of family therapy; these included Virginia Satir, Paul Watzlawick, and Jules Riskin, all leading figures in the development of the field. Bateson, however, was disenchanted with the new focus on clinical interventions. Never having seen himself primarily as an interventionist, Bateson moved outside the family therapy field and served as a philosopher interested in epistemology and ecology, inspiring a subsequent generation of environmentalists and ecologists (Broderick & Schrader, 1981; Lipset, 1982).

By the mid-1950s, a number of psychiatrists and other therapists outside the Mental Research Institute team were also experimenting with family therapy interventions, mostly based on a combination of psychoanalytic theory and newly developing systems principles. However, it was not until 1961 that most of these experimenters met and founded a new journal, *Family Process* (Broderick & Schrader, 1981). The founders included John Bell, Nathan Ackerman, Christian Midelfort, Theodore Lidz, Lyman Wynne, Murray Bowen, Carl Whitaker, James Framo, Jay Haley, John Weakland, Don Jackson, Virginia Satir, and Ivan Boszormenyi-Nagy. The effort to understand and treat schizophrenia was a common thread among these pioneer family therapists. Many combined research and clinical foci, a union that was lost during the burgeoning of the family therapy field during the 1970s (Wynne, 1983). Each used a unique vocabulary to describe family processes, and many developed a distinctive approach to clinical intervention. The result was a division of family therapy into theoretical and clinical schools or camps, a divergent process that continued until the 1980s when a second generation of family therapists began to assume leadership.

Murray Bowen

Out of the 1950s and 1960s, psychiatrist Murray Bowen emerged as the leading theoretician providing an alternative to Bateson's Palo Alto group, which developed theories of change in family therapy but deliberately avoided developing a more comprehensive theory about family process and family functioning (Watzlawick, Beavin, & Jackson, 1967). Although other family therapists were making important research and clinical contributions during this time, Bowen was the first to develop a comprehensive theory of family functioning (Bowen, 1978; Kerr & Bowen, 1988).

Bowen was the son of a funeral director and a member of complex, intertwined family in Tennessee. He was attracted to biology and evolutionary theory while training to be a psychiatrist. After initial training in psychoanalytic therapy, he began to become interested in families as a natural system. Bowen worked first at the Menninger Clinic in Kansas and then in 1954 moved to the National Institute of Mental Health where he conducted research on families and schizophrenia and began to develop his systems theory and therapy. In 1959 he moved to Georgetown Medical School and founded a family therapy training program that continues to bear his name.

In 1967, Bowen made the most famous public presentation in the history of family therapy. At a family therapy conference in Philadelphia, he presented a paper, "On the Differentiation of Self," which was a description of his own family and his efforts to become differentiated as an adult while still maintaining contact (Bowen, 1978). It was also a striking effort to differentiate his model as more than a technique of working with family of origin issues and to stake claim to the necessity of the therapist's own development.

Using a biological metaphor linking individual and family differentiation, Bowen's theory described how family processes foster or diminish the individual's differentiation of self to achieve of a balance between intellectual and emotional functioning and a balance of autonomy and togetherness in social relationships. Bowen viewed individuals as struggling with an evolutionary past from biology that accentuates lower brain functioning and stimulates fight-or-flight anxiety. Anxiety in turn leads to low differentiation of self or the inability to separate the emotional and rational domains of the mind. Anxiety and low differentiation of self are fostered in a nuclear family emotional system characterized by emotional fusion without autonomy, emotional cutoff out of fear of fusion, and conflict through third patties rather than directly (triangulation). In Bowen's theory, a family's problems with low differentiation between family members and with triangulation are apt to be transmitted to the next generation unless corrective measures are taken.

Bowen de-emphasized technique in his therapy model. The heart of therapeutic healing in Bowen family therapy is the therapist's own differentiation of self and consequent ability to stay out of triangles and to maintain a nonanxious objectivity in the face of the family's emotional field. The goal is to promote the differentiation of family members so that they can be distinct selves while maintaining emotional connection.

Assessment involves genograms that examine the emotional history of each family of origin. In therapy sessions the therapist focuses on the spouses (or a single parent or family leader) and controls the interchanges in therapy to diminish reactivity and to help them touch on areas of emotional importance in a calm, low-key way. The therapist's nonreactivity is crucial in modifying the emotional field. After the initial therapy phase that focuses on lowering reactivity, patients are coached to research their family of origin, focusing on issues such as locating cutoffs, finding lost relatives, correlating dates of change, delineating interlocking triangles, and noting similarities of symptoms, issues, and the positions of those who become symptomatic over the generations (Friedman, 1985). Patients ultimately are helped to change their responses to habitual family interactions, to maintain an "I" position that combines individuation and connection. In cases where patients have done good family work and anxiety is very low, Bowen would use later sessions for didactic explanations of the theory underlying the work.

Salvador Minuchin and Structural Family Therapy

Salvador Minuchin arguably had the greatest influence on the development of family therapy as an intervention. He grew up a Jewish Argentinean with a strong sense of kinship and a willingness to oppose established authorities. Trained originally in child psychoanalysis, Minuchin became disenchanted with this nonactivist way of working when he began working with low-income children at the Wiltwyck School for Boys in New York in the early 1960s. After becoming exposed to family systems theory through the Palo Alto group and other family therapy pioneers, Minuchin became a prominent figure in the field after 1965 when he became the first director of the Philadelphia Child Guidance Clinic, where Jay Haley joined him in the 1970s to create a powerhouse training program. Other key colleagues in Philadelphia were Braulio Montalvo, Harry Aponte, and Marianne Walters.

Minuchin's structural family therapy model arose during the early years of the community mental health movement and the antipoverty movement, which were attempts to create alternatives to hospital-based treatment and psychodynamic private practice treatment. Structural family therapy was developed from work with "under-organized" poor families by focusing on immediacy, on problem solving, and on the environmental context. The training model was practical and teachable, with an emphasis on direct observation and coaching behind one-way mirrors and video-taped review. The structural family therapy model was later extended to "over-organized" families of the middle class whose children developed disorders related to anorexia nervosa.

Minuchin emphasized the family as a system operating through sub-systems that require adequate boundary clarity and permeability. Minuchin proposed that families have functions, particularly socialization of children and mutual support of married couples, that are carried out through well-bounded subsystems. Thus, parents form an executive subsystem that is responsible for children; coalitions between a child and a parent against the other parent are inherently dysfunctional because they violate universal norms of power hierarchy in families.

In structural family therapy theory, families experience trouble when their boundaries are too porous (enmeshed) or too rigid (disengaged). The former prevents children from achieving autonomy and the latter prevents them from receiving enough support. All of these family dynamics are visible to the therapist who analyzes family interaction patterns. Minuchin was one of the pioneers, along with Lyman Wynne, who embraced a biopsychosocial model that allowed for the interplay of biology and family dynamics. In their classic work on children with brittle type I diabetes, Minuchin and his colleagues demonstrated how metabolic changes in children from certain kinds of enmeshed families are correlated with parental interactions. The "psychosomatic family" is characterized by a constellation of qualities whose description sums up the key initial contributions of structural family therapy to the field: enmeshed parent–child boundaries (overinvolved and hyper-responsive parenting), overprotection, rigidity, poor conflict resolution or conflict avoidance, triangulation (two family members aligning against a third one, especially when one parent forms a coalition with the child against the other parent), and detouring (when parents maintain a false solidarity in their own relationship by focusing on and thereby reinforcing the negative behavior of the child; Minuchin, Rosman, & Baker, 1978).

An additional important emphasis of structural family therapy stemmed from Minuchin's work with low-income urban families—that families can become dysfunctional in response to a hostile environment that overwhelms their adaptability. Adaptability, defined as the family's ability to access and execute alternative interactional patterns, becomes the "master trait" that determines how functional a family will remain in the face of major stressful events.

In its classic form as described by Minuchin (1974) the therapist's role is highly active, like a choreographer or director. The first phase of therapy is joining/accommodating: connecting with the family through politeness, confirming their feeling and fears, and initially showing respect for their transactional rules. The second phase is restructuring problematic family patterns through altering perceptions of the problem (such as de-emphasizing the symptom or relabeling it, for example, not as anxiety but as stubbornness); through enactments, which are in vivo experiences of an alternative family pattern (such as blocking interruptions, unbalancing coalitions, or enforcing boundaries between the generations); and task assignments for the home to stabilize the new patterns (such as assigning an uninvolved father the responsibility to eat meals with his anorexic daughter). One reason for the prominence of structural family therapy over the past four decades has been its straightforward set of practical strategies. Structural family therapy has changed over the years as Minuchin and his collaborators have developed interests in individuals in families and in larger systems, and it has influenced many other approaches to family therapy,

Strategic Family Therapy

The Palo Alto team developed its distinctive approach to therapy through the influence of Milton Erickson, the eminent hypnotherapist who focused on immediate change and idiosyncratic problem solving, not on personality or etiology of mental illness. He viewed symptoms as valuable forms of communication. Working by indirect suggestions, trance induction, and creating binds, Erickson fostered new beliefs in personal resources and personal flexibility.

By 1967 the Palo Alto team of Haley, Weakland, Watzlawick, and Bodin developed an amalgam of family systems theory, Ericksonian hypnotherapy, and constructivism (a focus on subjective perceptions of the world) into an approach they called brief therapy (Weakland, Fisch, Watzlawick, & Bodin, 1974). During the mid-1970s, Haley worked with Minuchin to form a hybrid of Ericksonian and structural family therapy, which became known as strategic family therapy, to which Chloe Madanes (1981) became a chief contributor.

In strategic family therapy, symptoms are seen as communicative, metaphorical acts involving a contract between two or more family members. They stem from impasses in the family's life and provide a way out. They also provide a way to protect or stabilize the family, as when a child acts out to distract the parents from their marital problems. Symptoms are also a way that individuals control the family, and, echoing Minuchin, symptoms often emerge from dysfunctional triangles that distort generational hierarchies in the family.

Strategic family therapists avoided diagnostic labels, believing that most problems persist through the mishandling of life's ordinary difficulties. People maintain problems by how they try to solve them, as when the pursuer keeps chasing the distancer or a spouse keeps trying to cheer up a depressed partner who has to demonstrate how terrible he or she really feels. Insight into one's past and one's inner motivations is not a prerequisite for change, although altered beliefs in self and family are important motivators for change.

In terms of intervention, strategic family therapy is directive and brief, aiming for rapid change. The therapist formulates a hypothesis about what is maintaining the problem—how the interpersonal world is organized around the symptom and the attempts to solve it—and then develops a plan for the most efficient way to bring about change. One universal intervention is reframing: altering perceptions of the problem by relabeling it (for example, school phobia is school refusal) or ascribing noble intentions (school refusal is a way to give Mom a reason to stay home and care for the child).

Strategic therapy is best known for paradoxical interventions. Sometimes the therapist might use the paradoxical technique of restraining change, urging the family to go slow with improving lest there be negative repercussions. This technique is intended to work creatively with the family's resistance to change. Sometimes the therapist might prescribe the symptom to make an involuntary behavior appear voluntary in a complex family dynamic. For example, the parents might encourage battling siblings to schedule prearranged fights or a child who is manipulating through physical symptoms to get sick at a particular time. The goal is 180-degree rapid change through breaking the lock that the symptom holds on the family.

Based on his work with Minuchin, Haley added to strategic family therapy an emphasis on working with malfunctioning hierarchies in families with disturbed late adolescents (Haley, 1976). This approach involves the parents taking charge and getting the adolescent back in the family through an empowered coparental alliance, and then increasingly allowing more independence as the adolescent's or young adult's behavior becomes normal. This is opposite the assumption among therapists that late adolescents should be treated individually and freed from parental control. Moreover, when progress is made, Haley assumed that the family would destabilize as the parents deal with their own issues, whereupon the therapist turns to help the parents. All of this work is done as quickly as possible, and the therapy ends with the therapist crediting the family for the change. Strategic family therapists want to avoid dependence of the family on the therapist.

Nowadays strategic family therapy is rarely practiced in its pure form in a therapy environment that emphasizes more collaborative engagement with families. But it gave the field powerful conceptual tools and ways of working with families that are part of the work of most contemporary family therapists.

OTHER FIRST GENERATION MODELS

Most of the founders of family therapy were originally trained in psychoanalysis, which was the centerpiece of psychotherapy in the mid-20th century. Nathan Ackerman (1958) was a key figure in developing a psychoanalytical model of family therapy and founding the Ackerman Family Institute in New York, which remains a prominent training center, albeit no longer psychoanalytical in orientation. Other first generation pioneers of family therapy influenced subsequent generations without founding models that became mainstream in the field. Prominent among these were Carl Whitaker and Virginia Satir, who emphasized (in different ways) the experiential and affective dimensions of family therapy, with the goal of greater personal growth and emotional depth. Experiential family therapists saw human growth and development with a family systems context, in the delicate dance of closeness and individual autonomy. Their intervention techniques emphasized a strong encounter between the therapist and the family, often escalating tension to produce breakthroughs.

Finally, behavioral family therapy was a late comer to the first generation of family therapy models. It was pioneered by Gerald Patterson (1971), who came from the tradition of social learning theory and behavioral theory as opposed to family systems theory. Patterson developed Parent Training, which went on to become one of the strongest, evidence-based models for treating children with behavioral problems. As a behaviorist, Patterson stressed the functional analysis of the dyadic interactions between a parent and child, looking for ways that negative behavior is reinforced through what follows it. He focused particularly on coercive control loops whereby the child gains the parent's attention primarily when she or he is acting out, and he helped parents emphasize positive reinforcement, incentive charts, and the use of less aversive and more effective management techniques such as time out. Over time, Patterson adopted a wider lens on family interactions beyond the parent–child dyad, and his work became more systemic. In more recent years, cognitive–behavioral therapy has become increasingly important in the treatment of marital and couples problems (Jacobson & Christensen, 1998) and has been integrated into a variety of contemporary evidence-based approaches to family therapy covered in chapter 5 of this volume.

THE SECOND GENERATION

In the late 1970s and 1980s, family therapists began to move away from adherence to a single founding model. At the same time, innovators were developing new models that went in two different directions: toward a leaner, less theory-driven approach that disdained the world of medicine and toward more integrative approaches that embraced collaborative practice with medicine.

Solution-Oriented Therapy

Solution-oriented therapy grew out of strategic family therapy, especially the move away of the MRI model from theory, family history, and psychopathology. Even more than strategic therapy, solution-oriented therapy eschewed theory about the origins of problems and instead focused on goals, resources, and exceptions to problem behavior, rather than on problems themselves. Reflecting a radical approach to constructivism (the idea that reality is socially created rather than mainly objective), solution-oriented therapists aimed for therapeutic conversations that construct alternative realities that would lead to quick problem resolution through activating patients' abilities. Leading figures were Steve de Shazer (1985), Insoo Berg, Eve Lipchick, and Michele Weiner-Davis (all connected with the Brief Therapy Center in Milwaukee), and Bill O'Hanlon of Omaha, who was trained by Milton Erickson (O'Hanlon & Weiner-Davis, 2003).

Solution-oriented therapy brought a number of innovative techniques into the field. In the miracle question, the therapist asks: "If you wake up one morning and a miracle has occurred and your problem is cured, how would you know it?" The patient is asked to elaborate the details—what would you and others in your family be doing differently if this miracle occurred. Then the therapist asks if there have there been any time recently when the miracle was present at least temporarily—for example, times when the patient was not drinking and was acting responsibly or the couple was getting along nicely. How would others in the patient's world know the miracle happened, and how would they be acting differently? The goal is to stimulate the imagination about change and instill hope.

Another prominent solution-oriented technique is scaling questions. Here's an example from Berg and Ruess (1998) in the substance abuse area. The therapist says to the patient: Let's say you have reasonable control over your substance use. If the number 1 stands for the time you lost complete control, where would you say you are at between 1 and 10 right now? What did you do to get from 1 to where you are now? What would you have to do to move up one step? The patient is then encouraged to think about and enact a simple behavior that would move to the next level of control over the symptomatic behavior. Solution-oriented therapists challenged the first generation of family therapists by arguing that no theoretical work is needed beyond a basic model of how people can activate themselves to change. Like strategic therapy, solution-oriented family therapy now is rarely practiced in its pure form in contemporary family therapy, but it has added greatly to the body of clinical strategies in the field.

Narrative Therapy

Postmodernism hit family therapy in the 1980s in the form of narrative therapy (Doherty, 1999). Narrative therapy critiqued theory and expert knowledge in favor of a constructivist emphasis on narrative, story, and the cocreation of reality. The leading figures were Lynn Hoffman, Harry Goolishian, Harlene Anderson, Tom Andersen (Norway), and especially Michael White and David Epston (Australia and New Zealand). It was probably the cutting-edge movement in family therapy in the 1990s. We will focus on White and Epston's version because it has been the most influential.

Although trained in family systems therapy, White and Epston (1990) came to embrace French philosopher Michel Foucault's critique of expert knowledge as oppressive. Like individual psychotherapy theories and diagnostic systems, family systems theory was seen as a "totalizing" framework created by experts and imposed on ordinary people. Narrative therapists see people as developing "problem-saturated descriptions" of their lives, which clinicians frequently reinforce through traditional diagnosis and problem-oriented treatment. The goal of therapy is to free people from oppressive stories in their lives, stories derived from the dominant culture (including therapy), which they have learned to describe their problems. For example, a patient who has been told that she has chronic depression may internalize this diagnosis and view depression as a dominant character in the story of her life. The therapist's job is to "deconstruct" this narrative and help the patient reclaim ownership of her life.

In this way of thinking, therapy becomes a form of conversation that involves "re-storying," in which patients locate and generate alternative narratives that create an altered sense of self that is separate from the problem. The therapist does not diagnose and attempts to not use a substantive theory beyond assumptions about the role of narratives in people's lives. Focusing on cultural scripts, White and Epston are explicitly multicultural, profeminist, progay, prolesbian, and opposed to social oppression in all its forms.

Narrative therapists de-emphasize technique but do have a number of common practices. The therapist maintains a positive, curious stance and is frequently impressed with what the patient offers up in therapy.

The therapist speaks of the problem in a distanced way to help the patient "externalize" the problem. The problem is referred to as a separate entity existing outside the patient and family, which may have gotten control of the person or family. The problem is the problem, and the person is the person. Therapy is mostly a series of questions exploring the problem's control of the family, how the family sometimes controls the problem ("exceptions" and "unique outcomes"). For example, the therapist might ask about situations in which the patient's depression was not in charge and how the patient managed to make that happen. (Note the similarity to solution-oriented therapy, with the difference that the narrative therapist has a larger model of cultural influences on problems.) The goal is to liberate the family from their constraining constructions so that they can create alternative ones, or "re-author" their lives.

More than any other model of family therapy, narrative therapists have incorporated community perspectives into their clinical models by emphasizing how problems and problem-saturated language are often founded in mainstream cultural beliefs and maintained by the language and practices of professionals in the community (Madigan & Epston, 1995; White & Epston, 1990). Narrative therapists have experimented with ways to access the social networks of patients and to assist them in making stands against the culture and the mainstream treatment system (Madigan & Epston, 1995; Walgrave & Temasese, 1993).

Narrative therapy presented a major challenge to the first generation of family therapy models and continues to be a prominent force in the U.S. family therapy field, although not in the pure form of its originators. For one thing, it is difficult to do therapy in the United States without accommodating to the DSM diagnostic system. At a larger level, Nichols (2008) has argued that narrative therapists, in reacting against the rigidities of the first generation of family therapy, adopted rigidities of their own, rejecting the purity of systems theory for the purity of a postmodernist, social constructionist perspective that eschewed both biology and family dynamics. Narrative therapy continues to evolve in ways that transcend these limitations while staying true to its core focus on collaborative treatment of problems in their cultural context.

Psychoeducation Family Therapy and Medical Family Therapy

Family therapy was originally created to treat schizophrenia, but this approach fell into disrepute after the double bind hypothesis for schizophrenia was unsupported and after no research support emerged for other family theories of the etiology of schizophrenia. There was also concern about blaming families for their children with mental illness. Subsequently twin studies and other biological studies established a strong biological factor in schizophrenia. But in the 1970s, many professionals were dissatisfied with the long-term results of drug-only treatment for schizophrenia (usually accompanied with some form of supportive individual psychotherapy). At the same time, deinstitutionalization policies left families burdened by care for their members with chronic mental illness. On the professional front, biopsychosocial explanations and multimodal therapies became more acceptable during the 1980s as the field of therapy moved away from single models.

A number of psychiatrists and other family therapists working in mental hospital settings followed up on clinical observations about family influences on relapse and rehospitalization among young adult schizophrenics. Major figures included Ian Faloon, William MacFarlane, Carol Anderson, and J. P. Leff (see a discussion of this work in chap. 5, this volume). They produced a series of studies showing that psychoeducational family treatment was effective in preventing relapse and rehospitalization among people with schizophrenia (Anderson, Reiss, & Hogarty, 1986).

These therapists and researchers accepted the biological base for major mental illness. Reflecting earlier work by Lyman Wynne, they viewed the family environment as important as a possible precipitant and as a risk or supportive factor for maintaining treatment gains. The theory behind psychoeducational family treatment centered on *expressed emotion*, or critical overinvolvement of parents vis à vis their children with mental illness. As measured by the Camberwell Family Interview, expressed emotion was found to predict relapse and rehospitalization in schizophrenia.

Family psychoeducation works with individual families but is mostly done with family groups of relatives of the patient. The therapists present to families the biological theory of serious mental illness, along with findings for how families can best cope. They help families to learn low-key, nonreactive limit setting and problem solving, along with other behavioral strategies to support a healthy family environment. This treatment is combined with medication, social/vocational, and community-based interventions. Family psychoeducation for serious mental illness has an anomalous status in the field today: It is the best validated family treatment for serious mental disorder, and yet it is not widely practiced in psychiatric settings that are dominated by medical treatments.

Like family psychoeducation, medical family therapy embraces a biopsychosocial framework for health problems: body, mind, family, community, and wider environments. With roots in earlier work by pioneers such as Wynne and Minuchin, medical family therapy was crystallized by family therapists in the 1980s who worked in medical settings. The authors of this book were among a group that included Jeri Hepworth, John Rolland, Alexander Blount, and others. The term *medical family therapy* was originally coined by McDaniel, Hepworth, and Doherty in their 1992 book of that name. The authors criticized the family therapy field for abandoning early efforts (by Bateson, Bowen, Wynne, Minuchin, and others) to understand how biology works with family systems. Medical family therapy expanded the scope of family therapy beyond work with mental health problems to include the whole scope of health problems, especially chronic medical illness. Like other medical family therapists, McDaniel, Hepworth, and Doherty (1992) emphasized close collaborative work between therapists, physicians, and other providers. They formulated goals of this work as promoting agency and communion (autonomy and connectedness) in patients, families, and provider systems.

Medical family therapy is a *metamodel*, which means it is an overarching framework within which a therapist can use her or his preferred therapy model. This overarching framework emphasizes taking medical illness seriously instead of perpetuating the mind–body split; taking families seriously as a locus of health, illness, and coping; and seeing oneself as working as part of a team of multidisciplinary providers rather than a solo operator or part of a mental health team.

There were other important developments in second generation family therapy that did not lead to specific or enduring therapy models. For example, the Milan model of family therapy flourished for a time as a further development of strategic family therapy. It influenced leaders in the field but did not endure as a therapy model (Selvini- Palazzoli, Boscolo, Cecchin, & Prata, 1980). Of special note is feminist family therapy, which emerged during the 1980s as a critique of male-oriented assumptions in the first generation models (Goldner, 1986). Feminists pointed out that the field came slowly to be influenced by second wave feminism and therefore carried biases about male power and female subordination in families and in the therapy room. They also noted the shortage of prominent women leaders in the field, a problem that was corrected in the decade of the 1990s. While not leading to a specific model of feminist family therapy, this second generation development has had a strong and enduring impact on the field.

THIRD GENERATION

Contemporary family therapists are more integrative and eclectic than their forebears, and emerging models reflect this shift. Two research-based, integrative family therapy models have become prominent in the treatment of children and adolescents with serious behavioral problems. They use many of the first and second generation family therapy tools but add an ecological perspective by working with multiple systems in the child's life. They are also more explicitly research and evidence based.

Multisystemic Therapy

Multisystemic therapy was created by Henggeler and colleagues in the 1990s as a way to work with highly challenging child and adolescent problems (Henggeler & Sheidow, 2002). The model was drawn from a wide range of theories: structural family therapy, strategic family therapy, cognitive–behavioral theories, and socioecological theories. It is a home-based approach in which the therapist works with the family and community systems to reduce crime, substance abuse, and other problems that threaten an out-of-home placement. The therapist works with sometimes divergent goals of multiple systems and brings them into alignment around the goal of the child's success. With the family, the therapist is persistent (not giving up on noncooperative families) and goal and action oriented, working with specific tasks and interaction sequences that are tailored to each family. Multisystemic therapy has achieved substantial research support and is becoming widely adopted by government and agency groups around the country.

Multidimensional Family Therapy

Multidimensional family therapy was developed by Howard Liddle, who trained originally as a structural and strategic family therapist, to treat entrenched problems of adolescent substance abusers (Liddle et al., 2001). Like multisystemic therapy, it has achieved success with low-income, highly challenged families. Deliberately integrative of several family therapy and ecological models, multidimensional family therapy is based on the premise that complex problems require interventions with multiple systems of development and influence: the adolescent, the parents, the family, and community systems. Careful attention is paid to joining with the adolescent as an individual (note the greater emphasis on the individual than in first generation family therapy models) and with the parents before engaging other systems. There is a focus on behavioral management and affective ties in the family. Multidimensional family therapy developed as a research model of treatment and, unlike multisystemic therapy, has only recently been extended to community settings.

Other evidence-based family therapy models have gained increased attention in recent years. Functional family therapy was developed by family psychologist James Alexander to treat behavior problems in children (Sexton & Alexander, 2002). Cognitive–behavioral approaches to family therapy have brought an empirically rich tradition from individual psychotherapy to family therapy (Dattilio & Epstein, 2004). Finally, although marriage and couples therapy models are outside the purview of this book, two contemporary models deserve mention: cognitive–behavioral couples therapy and emotion-focused couples therapy. Pioneered by Weiss, Jacobson, Margolin, and Christensen, cognitive–behavioral couples therapy aims to decrease blame, increase positive behaviors, and teach empathy and constructive problem solving (Jacobson & Margolin, 1979). Emotion-focused couples therapy, developed by Susan Johnson and Les Greenberg, applies attachment theory to treating couples (Johnson, 1996). With a strong emphasis on emotional states, it involves a structured three-stage process: de-escalation of conflict, restructuring the attachment bond between the partners, and consolidating gains. Since many family therapists work with couples as well as intergenerational families (and individuals), these two evidence-based models of couples therapy have become increasingly important in the family therapy field.

CONCLUSION

The history of family therapy has been noteworthy for its innovators and strong, charismatic personalities. The pioneers were mavericks and rebels against psychoanalysis, bringing in strange theories from biology and cybernetics and claiming that it is better to work with families than individuals. Many of the founders divided into different schools and trained disciples. The second generation also were rebels, with one group trying to purify family therapy of any thinking that was not needed to make change, a second group claiming that the first generation models were oppressive, and a third group calling the field back to a biopsychosocial approach. The third generation did not begin with critique but with an effort to do two new things: combine elements of existing models to work with defined populations and combine research and clinical practice from the outset. Pervading all three generations is a set of powerful ideas about families and human problems, and a set of innovative ways to approach these problems. These are the focus of the next two chapters.

3

Theory

The goal of most theories in family therapy is to explain how psychological and relationship problems emerge from the functioning and dynamics of family systems. Notice that we say "emerge from" rather than "caused by." The reason is that systems theory avoids the language of linear causality—one cause creating one effect—in favor of a more complex understanding that is closer to how dance partners influence each other: There is the couple dancing, the other dancers around them, the music, and the environment. All the elements together are necessary to explain what goes well or poorly for the dancing partners. Later we will discuss how the initial focus on internal family dynamics led to later thinking about the role of larger systems in individual and relationship problems. But first we focus on the fundamental questions and classic concepts laid out by the founders of family therapy.

Portions of this chapter are adapted from "Theories Emerging From Marriage and Family Therapy," by W. J. Doherty and D. Baptiste, 1993, in P. G. Boss, W. J. Doherty, R. LaRossa, S. K. Steinmentz, and W. R. Schumm (Eds.), *Sourcebook of Family Theories and Methods: A Contextual Approach* (pp. 505–529), New York: Plenum. Copyright 1993 by Springer. Reprinted with permission.

CLASSIC QUESTIONS ADDRESSED
BY FAMILY THERAPY THEORY

Every theory has a set of driving questions it attempts to answer, and as theories develop over time, they usually extend their reach as new questions arise. Here are the original questions addressed by family therapy theories.

1. *How do individuals develop symptoms within families?* This was the primary question in the development of family therapy, with the initial focus on schizophrenia and then on a wide range of psychosocial problems, including depression, anxiety disorders, psychosomatic illness, childhood conduct disorders, and substance abuse disorders. When a "new" problem was identified, such as bulimia and borderline personality disorder, family therapy theorists set about understanding the problem in terms of its family context. Sometimes the emphasis is on how family dynamics lead to the onset of a particular problem (such as oppositional defiant disorder stemming from undermining between the parents), and sometimes the emphasis is on how the family comes to organize itself around the disorder and thereby perpetuate the problem (as in the case of anxiety disorders or alcoholism in which the disorder might have preceded the formation of the family but family dynamics keep it going). All family therapy theories place a major emphasis on here-and-now family process, while some also emphasize longer-term family of origin processes.

2. *How do families maintain levels of interpersonal connection that allow for both emotional bonding and individual autonomy?* Different theorists address this question in different ways. Bowen (1978) viewed the family as tending toward interpersonal enmeshment or overinvolvement; optimal functioning involves the fostering of differentiation of self and consequent ability to maintain emotional connections without loss of autonomy. Minuchin (1974) viewed the family as tending toward extremes of enmeshment or disengagement, with the former promoting family cohesion at the expense of the individual and the latter promoting the opposite. Minuchin also emphasized the importance of differentiated subsystems in the family; for example, a clear but flexible boundary separating the parental subsystem from the children's subsys-

tem promotes separation within the context of interpersonal support. We will discuss the term *boundary* more fully later in this chapter.

3. *How does family conflict become unmanageable?* For obvious reasons, family conflict is a major preoccupation of family therapy theories. A core approach to understanding family conflict relies on systems dynamics first identified by Bateson in the 1930s: the circular processes whereby negative interactions escalate symmetrically to destructive levels (Watzlawick et al., 1967). For example, a father's coerciveness elicits rebellious responses by his son, which leads to further coerciveness from the father and heightened resistance from the son—and so the escalation continues. A second standard approach is to examine the role of third parties (triangular patterns) in maintaining irresolvable conflicts. A covert alliance between mother and son might underlie the sustained, overt conflict between father and son (Haley, 1976). A third approach to the question of unmanageable family conflict focuses on overall family systems properties such as overconnectedness or enmeshment, which would make serious conflict flow from attempts of family members to assert and protect their autonomy (Minuchin, 1974).

4. *How can families change dysfunctional patterns?* Here the primary focus has been on how therapists can assist families to change. Family therapists generally view the unit of systems change as one consisting of a therapist and a family (Haley, 1976). The therapist uses the therapeutic relationship to elicit new family patterns, which the family internalizes at home. Chapter 4 of this volume covers the major mechanisms of change in family therapy.

Dozens of other important questions about families are addressed by theory in family therapy. However, we think that most of them can be subsumed under the four we have delineated here.

CLASSIC CONCEPTS

Relatively few concepts are employed in all family therapy theories. Nevertheless, a number of concepts are in common parlance because of their status as classic, first generation family therapy ideas. Later we will address newer and emerging concepts. Although there are formal assessment tools for these and other family therapy concepts (Jordin, 2003), the complexity of family dynamics is such that few assessment tools can capture the subtleties of a particular family. Here we stress how family therapists see the family dynamics emerging in the clinical interview from history and direct observation of families in the therapy room.

1. *Cohesion and individuation.* Implicit or explicit in every theory of family functioning that has arisen from family therapy is the idea that optimal family functioning involves a precarious balance between group solidarity, often termed cohesion, and individual autonomy, often called differentiation (Olson, Russell, & Sprenkle, 1983). Families with too much connectedness raise children who are oversocialized and have difficulty leaving home emotionally, and families with too much separateness raise children who are undersocialized and will have difficulty trusting others (Minuchin, 1974). In both cases, it is considered likely that some family members will show signs of psychosocial pathology.

Determining a family's levels of cohesion and individuation cannot be done without an understanding of the family's cultural context (McGoldrick, Giordano, & Garcia-Preto, 2005) and life cycle stage (Carter & McGoldrick, 2005). Some families are more intensely involved with one another as a reflection of their ethnicity, and families with young children are likely to be more engaged with one another than families with young adult offspring. What family therapists look for are struggles over connection and autonomy (such as parent–adolescent conflict over rules), lack of nurturance and support for a dependent family member (such an ill member who is not being cared for adequately), and the inability of a family member to make decisions and play independent roles in his or her cultural context (as when a young adult is not able to make friends and secure employment). In the therapy room, enmeshment can be seen in family members speaking for one another and reading one another's minds. Disengagement can be seen in family members' not responding to emotional cues and failing to connect with the process of healing and change.

2. *Adaptability*. Derived from the systems theory principle that successful organisms are continually adapting to their environment, the concept of family adaptability or flexibility is a cornerstone of family therapy theory (von Bertalanffy, 1976). It means the ability of a family to shift its beliefs and interactional styles in the face of developmental changes and environmental challenges that can create relational problems and psychosocial pathology in family members. In articulating their circumplex model of family assessment, Olson, Russell, and Sprenkle (1983) maintain that adaptability (flexibility) and cohesion (connectedness versus separateness) are the two primary concepts in all systems theories of the family.

   Family therapists see adaptability in how the family has coped with challenges in the past and how it rises to the challenge presented in therapy now. In adjusting to a divorce, some families form workable new patterns of shared parenting in different households, while others become paralyzed around coparental conflict and resistance of children to change. In dealing with a serious illness in an elderly parent, some families take on and share new caregiver roles, while in other families one child steps up while the others continue to relate to the parent as if nothing has changed.

3. *Boundaries*. This concept, which is most widely used in structural family therapy (Minuchin, 1974), has roots in systems theory. Every living organism has boundaries separating it from its environment, and complex organisms have internal boundaries demarcating subsystems such as cells and organs (von Bertalanffy, 1976). Minuchin defined boundaries as family rules determining who will participate in the family and its subsystems and how they will participate. Boundaries must be clear if family members are to know how to relate to one another and to the world. As described previously, family boundaries can be enmeshed—not enough protection of autonomy—or disengaged to the exclusion of appropriate contact between members of different subsystems. Pauline Boss's (2001) research demonstrates the consequences of this "boundary ambiguity," when family members are unclear as to who is in and out of the family and its subsystems. Clear boundaries also protect the

integrity of subsystems within the family such as the marital couple or the sibling group. They also allow for a balance of cohesion and individuation.

Family therapists see boundary violations in situations such as a father sharing confidences with his daughter about his relationship with the mother, or when an adolescent boy becomes a quasi-spouse to his mother after the death of the father. Therapists see boundary ambiguity in situations when it's not clear whether a new stepparent is a "real" parent with authority or just the spouse of the real parent. In general, boundaries are one of the most useful concepts in family therapy.

4. *Triangles*. Triadic interactional configurations are at the heart of how family therapists think about problematic family interactions. Bowen (1978) defined a triangle as a ""three-person emotional configuration" and saw triangles as the basic building block of any emotional system, including the family. Bowen proposed that two person systems become unstable in the face of high anxiety, leading them to involve a third party—often the most vulnerable family member—to form a more stable triangle. For example, destabilizing marital conflict might become deflected into disagreement over parenting, with the child's problems keeping the focus away from the original marital problem. This triangle endures during calmer periods, with emotional forces continually shifting back and forth among the threesome. In subsequent periods of high stress, according to Bowen, each family member tries for the outside position, leaving the conflict to be contained between the other two.

Family therapists see Bowen-type triangles in situations where a father might take the outside position during family conflict, leaving the arguments to occur between mother and child. In one case, the 12-year-old boy would curse his mother (but never his father) when he got angry at her, while the father stayed "neutral" and disengaged. Family therapists often focus on family secrets as a way to understand emotional triangles in a family—who is in the know on a family secret and who is cut out, and then who takes the heat when the secret is revealed.

5. *Coalitions*. This is a variation, out of structural and strategic family therapy, on the triangle concept that emphasizes negative alliances,

termed coalitions, between two or more family members against another family member. Some coalitions involve the basic three parties in a triad, whereas other coalitions can involve larger groups, as when several adult children align with father in blaming mother for a parental divorce. The term *coalition* was used extensively by Minuchin (1974) in his discussion of three kinds of "rigid family triads." The first rigid triad, called *triangulation*, is the pattern in which a parent demands that the child take sides in a parental dispute. The second concept, *detouring*, is the pattern whereby parents maintain harmony by reinforcing a child's deviant behavior; focusing on the child's problems allows them to avoid dealing with their own conflict. Finally, intergenerational coalitions are deemed by Minuchin (1974), Haley (1976), and many other theorists to be a central dysfunctional pattern in families. These occur most commonly when one parent and a child take sides against another parent. This pattern can continue throughout life.

Family therapists see coalitions when a divorced mother tells her children that their (good enough) father cannot be trusted, when a father tells his adult daughter that her mother was never "affectionate" enough for him, and when an out-of-town daughter works with a frail parent to prevent a nursing home placement by allying behind the back of the in-town daughter who is responsible for the mother's care.

6. *Intergenerational transmission.* A key principle of family therapy is that family interaction patterns tend to repeat across generations and may create problems for subsequent generations. While no family therapy theory would dispute this assumption, several theories strongly emphasize it. These include Bowen's theory (Bowen, 1978; Kerr & Bowen, 1988) and Boszormenyi-Nagy's theory of the family as an ethical group (Boszormenyi-Nagy & Spark, 1973). Boszormenyi-Nagy, for example, described how "destructive entitlement" is passed on through generations when a child who feels deprived of attentive, responsible parenting grows up with a sense of being owed by the world and becomes an inattentive, nonresponsible parent to the next generation. Bowen described how patterns of "cutoffs" between family members can take hold over many generations as family

members deal with their anxiety and conflict by amputating family relationships.

Family therapists often see intergenerational patterns of cutoffs between fathers and children, based in part on the fragility of male–female couple relationships. This challenge is especially common among low-income families facing employment and other environmental challenges (Edin & Kefalas, 2007). Despite feeling hurt by the underinvolvement of their fathers, children grow up to expect and repeat the pattern.

7. *Family belief systems.* Family therapists have always been concerned with how family members understand their problems. But it was not until the 1970s and 1980s that theories developed a more explicit emphasis on family beliefs systems. Kantor and Lehr (1975) and Constantine (1986) presented a theory of family paradigms, which are a family's fundamental worldview—its core beliefs and values about how the family should function. For example, how does the family view the larger world—as a safe place for the family interact with via open boundaries or a dangerous place to be walled off as much as possible? The Milan model of family therapy developed an emphasis on particular family beliefs about the disturbed family member's symptom (Boscolo, Cecchin, Hoffman, & Penn, 1987). For example, adherents to the Milan model might hypothesize that family beliefs related to a child's obesity (family members agree he's just like his dad) may be tied into family dynamics that maintain the weight problem.

    Nowadays many therapists encounter differences between Western beliefs in mental health and those of non-Western immigrant families who view mental health problems as threatening and stigmatized in their communities. The advantage of seeing these beliefs as not just those of individuals but also of their families and communities is that the therapist is less apt to make the mistake of thinking that an individual family member can readily take on a new perspective. Forming a consensus with a family that its member's condition involves both emotional and physical components requires a respect for the power of family belief systems.

8. *Self processes.* This concept divides the family therapy field into two groups: those with an explicit theory of the self in addition to family process and those who remain exclusively at the level of family process. The major approaches to understanding the self in the family are object relations family therapy and Bowen's family therapy. James Framo (1981) was a pioneer in applying psychoanalytically derived object relations theory to family therapy. Object relations theory emphasizes how the self develops in relation to significant others, especially parents (see also Scharff & Scharff, 1987). Problematic parent–child relations lead to internal splits in the child (for example, good–bad, pride–shame) that are projected onto love objects as an adult. Thus, adult family members tend to see each other through lenses distorted by undeveloped parts of the self, which leads to efforts to turn each other into ideal parents who can complete the self. Idealization ends in disillusionment when the individual projects the disowned part of the self onto the family member. For example, a husband who is cut off from his own feelings of weakness and inadequacy projects them onto his wife and then tries to "fix" him by "fixing" her.

In Bowen's theory, self-differentiation is the psychological prerequisite for healthy family functioning. Only a differentiated self can handle constructively the emotional intensity of family relations, without resorting to reactive or disengaged behavior. This differentiation process involves the progressive ability to separate thinking from emotional process and to maintain one's capacity to make free choices in social situations involving strong affect.

Family therapists are always working with multiple "selves" in the family, and therefore have working models of the role of the self. But family therapists see the self in interpersonal terms, never an "I" separate from a "we." The internal splits of the self are highly visible in the therapy room and thus can be worked with directly, as when successful parents of a struggling young adult child project their fears of failure onto the offspring—and do so right in the therapy hour where the therapist can help them own their fears. When the parents bounce back and forth between overprotection and desire to cut their child off from the family, the family therapist can work on their differentiation of self—how to be in supportive relationship with their child without fusion or disengagement. Richard Schwarz (1997) developed a model of internal family systems therapy where the therapist uses systemic principles to work with multiple "parts" of the individual patient's self that frequently mirror interpersonal conflicts.

9. *Family life cycle challenges.* All family interaction patterns occur in the context of where the family is in its life course, from a family in formation to a family in old age, rearing children versus launching children, divorcing and recombining in stepfamilies, and so forth. In the early decades of family therapy, family life cycle stage was an implicit rather explicit emphasis. The work of Betty Carter and Monica McGoldrick (2005) brought work of family development scholars (Duvall, 1977; Hill, 1970) into the family therapy field. For example, it is not surprising that many families present for therapy when children are adolescents and the family is dealing with the challenge of managing to stay connected with parental leadership during a time when the adolescent requires more autonomy. Similarly, combining two families with children in a stepfamily poses challenges that tax the ability of families to change while maintaining continuity with the past.

The original family life cycle models focused on the stages of the nuclear family, but the same ideas can be applied to the complexities of extended families. It is not uncommon in today's world of longevity for therapists to work with four-generational families where one of the generations is attending to the needs of three others! One family, for example, had a stressful nursing placement of the great grandmother at the same time as a heart problem in her son in the next generation and a difficult pregnancy and health complication in the third generation, with a new baby in the fourth generation requiring extra attention because of an ill mother. Understanding the life cycle stages clashing here can be essential for the family therapist. Otherwise, the problems are seen as piecemeal and treated accordingly.

MORE RECENT CONCEPTS

Family therapy has expanded along with new social awareness about gender and culture. It has gone back to its roots in looking at the connection between biology and family systems. It also has expanded its scope to look at community influences and larger systems. One reason the field has been able to grapple successfully with this emergent spectrum of issues stems from its roots in systems theory—once you grasp how systems work, it's not a big leap from the family to larger systems and from the family to smaller, biological systems.

10. *Gender and family systems.* Traditional family systems theory and family therapy theories ignored gender in describing families. As Goldner (1988) pointed out in a pioneering article, family therapy theories have tended to focus only on generation, to the exclusion of gender. Beginning in the 1980s feminist family therapists contended that gender is a fundamental organizing principle of family systems; any theory lacking a model for gender is thereby impoverished theoretically—men and women have different experiences in family life as elsewhere—and is likely to ignore the social realities of gender hierarchy and balance of power in families. Feminist family therapists offered a thoroughgoing critique of the established theories in the field and put gender into every subsequent theoretical and clinical development (Goodrich, Rampage, Ellman, & Halstead, 1988; Hare-Mustin, 1986).

A gender lens has helped family therapists acknowledge that women, as most often the primary caregivers in families, are the ones who most often present for therapy. They are also likely to be faulted for the family's problems unless the therapist understands the larger social context of gender in families and the larger culture. It's tempting for the therapist, especially when working with single-parent families, to assign the father the role of "not in the picture" and assign all the responsibility to the mother. The same occurs with women as caregivers for ill family members.

11. *Race, ethnicity, and families.* Like gender, race and ethnicity were not prominent conceptual categories in the early decades of family therapy (just as they were not for most psychotherapy models). Thus, family therapy theory embraced what Kenneth Hardy (1989) termed "the theoretical myth of sameness," the idea that all families are more or less the same. This critique and a flood of literature, including McGoldrick, Pearce, and Giordano's (1982) *Ethnicity and Family Therapy* and Boyd-Franklin's (1989) *Black Families in Therapy,* opened up creative directions on understanding the role of cultural meanings in families, including how families define problems and how they relate to outside helpers. It also opened up family therapy theory even more to the influence of the social environment in which families of color live, a social environment that is likely to be marked by higher levels of poverty and unemployment, poorer educational opportunities, and greater exposure to crime. Ignoring the contribution of poverty and discrimination to family problems not only omits important explanatory concepts but also leads to an overestimation of the explanatory value of traditional family therapy concepts focusing on intrafamilial interaction patterns. As the United States becomes an increasingly pluralistic society, multicultural ideas and practices are seen as essential for the field.

    As family therapists work with more families where English is not the first language, they can apply their understanding of family dynamics such as generational boundaries to situations where the children speak English and the parents do not. Family therapists learn to be mindful of the problem of generational reversal when the children become the spokespersons and mediators between parents and professionals. Such boundary confusion, while sometimes unavoidable, is fraught with dangers for the children and the whole family.

12. *Families and larger systems.* Gender and race/ethnicity concepts emphasize the family in its larger environment. They force the therapist and theorist to scan a horizon beyond the therapy room and beyond the family's home. In parallel fashion during the 1980s came a renewed emphasis on understanding how families

interact with their immediate social environments. The core premise underlying work on families and larger systems has been that families are constituted, in part, by their interactions with major environmental systems such as health care, schools, justice and law enforcement systems, and mental health and social service systems. Thus, understanding family problems—the hallmark of family therapy theory—requires a way to analyze family transactions with the institutional environment. As a corollary, family treatment often requires intervention and collaboration with the major institutions immediately impinging on the family. Evan Imber-Black (1988) in her book *Families and Larger Systems* was one of the pioneers in applying family systems concepts to family–institutional relationships—concepts such as triangles, coalitions, boundaries, and belief systems. Families dealing with community institutions are expected to have more porous external boundaries than other families; their zone of privacy is limited, and there are many professional authority figures in the lives of the children. Imber-Black observed that there is often a mirroring (in systems terms, an isomorphism) between interaction processes at the family level, at the level of family interactions with community institutions, and even at the level of community institutions interactions with one another. An example offered by Imber-Black is a welfare family whose therapist wanted to enhance the parents' choices and whose welfare worker wanted to remove the children from the home. The family became "triangled" into this larger system conflict and became demoralized in the process.

The development of theory to understand the connections between the family and larger systems has become quite fruitful for the field, as shown in the development of areas such as medical family therapy (McDaniel et al., 1992), collaborative family health care (Blount, 1998), and systems consultation (Wynne, McDaniel, & Weber, 1986).

13. *Biopsychosocial systems.* As mentioned in chapter 2 of this volume, although many of the pioneers in the field were trained in biological medicine and were interested in the relationship of biology to

family life, theorists for the most part did not follow up on these leads. This neglect of biology changed when family therapists began to work in the burgeoning field of family medicine in the 1980s. Working alongside medical doctors and nurses, it was no longer possible for family therapists to ignore the role of physical illness such as cancer, diabetes, and heart disease on family functioning and how family process influenced the course of these illnesses (Doherty & Baird, 1983; McDaniel et al., 1992; Rolland, 1994). Family therapists adopted George Engel's (1977) biopsychosocial model, which proposed that all health and illness occurs in the context of biological, psychological, and social factors. They added family systems ideas that focus on the interactional patterns within families and between families and health care providers and larger systems. The result for family therapy was an expanded scope of understanding of human problems beyond the psychosocial or mental illness frame into the whole spectrum of biopsychosocial issues.

Once family therapists reopened the realm of biology, they began to see that diabetes and depression frequently go together in adults, and that both can be accompanied by marital or couple problems. Family therapists can use an assessment framework that includes an understanding of how all three problems influence one another and how the individual and family are embedded in a complex web of relationships with health care professionals.

14. *Expressed emotion.* As mentioned previously, family therapy was developed in large part by trying to understand the psychosocial origins of schizophrenia. This effort for the most part was abandoned when the medical model of schizophrenia became dominant after the introduction of antipsychotic medications. However, in the 1980s a new family systems concept, accompanied by potent research, entered the field. The idea of expressed

emotion was developed to understand how family interactions influence the course, not the cause, of schizophrenia. Expressed emotion is generally defined as the level of criticalness and emotional overinvolvement of a family member in relationship with another family member who has a psychiatric impairment such as schizophrenia or bipolar illness (Leff & Vaughn, 1985). Stated differently, expressed emotion is a form of negative enmeshment. It has been found in many research studies to lead to high risk for relapse and rehospitalization among people with serious mental illness, schizophrenia in particular. A key indicator of high levels of expressed emotion is the family member's spontaneous use of critical comments about the patient, such as "He is lazy" or "She will never grow up." The resulting negative atmosphere in the family is viewed as a risk for poor recovery from a psychotic episode. We will cover research on the treatment for expressed emotion in a latter section of this book.

THE FAMILY GENOGRAM

The family genogram is a valuable way to pull together many of the family therapy assessment concepts into a visual map. Many family therapists use genograms to collect and organize information across three or more generations, beginning with basic demographic information about family membership, marriages, divorces, deaths, adoptions, and miscarriages. The therapist can then add important family systems material such as cutoffs, conflictual and distant relationships, and enmeshed relationships. Depending on the clinical setting and the therapist's interests, other information can be added on mental and medical illnesses, behavioral health problems, religion, and many other factors. Figure 3.1 presents elements most commonly used to construct genograms. Chapter 4 of this volume has a genogram for a family therapy case along with a discussion of how it is used with families. In recent years family therapists have expanded on family genograms to include the wider community (Rigazio-DiGilio, Ivey, Kunkler-Peck, & Grady, 2005).

Figure 3.1

Genogram Format

A. Symbols to describe basic family membership and structure (include on genogram significant others who lived with or cared for family members — place them on the right side of the genogram with a notation about who they are.)

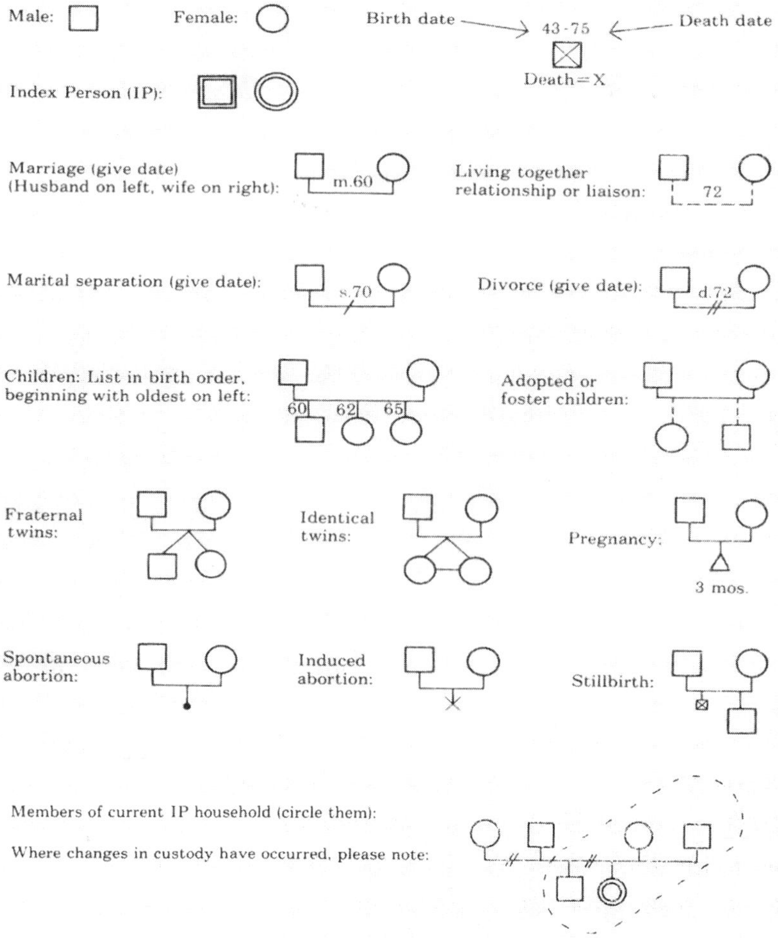

Male: ☐   Female: ◯   Birth date ⟶ 43-75 ⟵ Death date

Index Person (IP):   Death = X

Marriage (give date)   Living together
(Husband on left, wife on right):   m.60   relationship or liaison: 72

Marital separation (give date):   s.70   Divorce (give date):   d.72

Children: List in birth order,   Adopted or
beginning with oldest on left: 60| 62| 65| foster children:

Fraternal twins: Identical twins: Pregnancy: 3 mos.

Spontaneous abortion: Induced abortion: Stillbirth:

Members of current IP household (circle them):

Where changes in custody have occurred, please note:

Figure 3.1 (*Continued*)

B. Family interaction patterns. The following symbols are optional. The clinician may prefer to note them on a separate sheet. They are among the least precise information on the genogram, but may be key indicators of relationship patterns the clinician wants to remember:

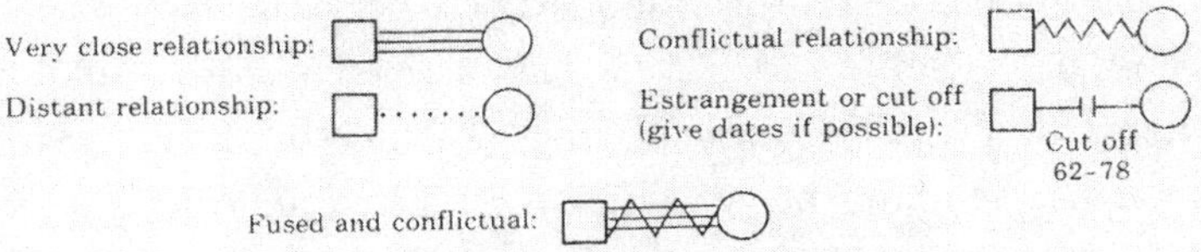

Very close relationship:

Distant relationship:

Conflictual relationship:

Estrangement or cut off (give dates if possible):
Cut off
62-78

Fused and conflictual:

C. Medical history. Since the genogram is meant to be an orienting map of the family, there is room to indicate only the most important factors. Thus, list only major or chronic illnesses and problems. Include dates in parentheses where feasible or applicable. Use DSM-III categories or recognized abbreviations where available (e.g., cancer: CA; stroke: CVA).

D. Other family information of special importance may also be noted on the genogram:

   1) Ethnic background and migration date
   2) Religion or religious change
   3) Education
   4) Occupation or unemployment
   5) Military service
   6) Retirement
   7) Trouble with law
   8) Physical abuse or incest
   9) Obesity
   10) Smoking
   11) Dates when family members left home: LH '74.
   12) Current location of family members

CONCLUSION

Family therapy has a rich conceptual history going back to the mid-1950s and continuing to develop today. Pinning down these nuanced concepts in empirical research has been difficult, although progress has been made in the last two decades (see chap. 5, this volume). Many family therapy ideas cannot be fully grasped cognitively without experience seeing families in the therapy room or the home. A dance can be described in words, but it has to be seen in action with the music playing. The concept of triangulation becomes real to a therapist when you are sitting with a couple or family and feel yourself being inducted into a coalition of one family member against another—the very pattern the family members enact with one another at home. It can happen in an instant, as when you make an observation to one family member that another member jumps on with vigorous agreement, thereby angering the first family member who fights back against you and your observation. This becomes valuable experiential information as you work with the family.

Of course, the other way to internalize family therapy ideas is to examine one's own family. In fact, experiential courses on family of origin are common in family therapy training programs, where trainees create their family genograms, investigate family history, interview relatives, and present their family story to their colleagues. We're reasonably sure that readers have been thinking of their own family systems throughout this chapter. Indeed, our own families are in the room every time we meet with a family, so it's a good idea to know where we are coming from!

4

The Therapy Process

With history and theory as a backdrop, this chapter describes the elements of family therapy and puts them into motion. It focuses on what family therapy looks like on the ground as a therapeutic approach and on how it changes individuals, families, and sometimes even professionals. As with other chapters in this book, we use a broad brush stroke to explain ways of working across the prominent models of family therapy.

APPLICATION OF FAMILY SYSTEMS THEORY

Family therapy can seem complex because of its attention to the many systems that contribute to who a patient is and with what he or she presents. We present here some examples of ways to apply family systems therapy as well as some illustrations of key concepts in the therapy process, such as *triangulation* and the dynamic of the *pursuer–distancer* in relationships.

The Patient's Symptom as a Function of Unresolved Family Issues

Family systems theory is based on the idea that an individual's symptoms are either a product of, or reinforced by, the interpersonal environment. Sometimes these patterns grow out of recent unresolved conflict; at other times they are the product of years, even generations, of problematic coping.

Consider this case example: Diana[1] was 18 when she and her 2-year-old daughter, Donna, were brought to therapy by her Irish-American mother, Debra, and stepfather, Don. When asked the problem, Diana said: "I don't know (nodding to her parents). They insist I come. I don't have any problems. I just want to spend time with my friends."

This answer provoked a strong response from her mother: "Diana, you gave up the chance to have an easy time of it when you got pregnant. You have a daughter now!" To the therapist, Diana's mother said: "We didn't ask for this. Diana got herself in trouble, and now she won't pay her dues. All she does is party, and I, for one, am unwilling to do all the babysitting. We love our granddaughter, but we've already raised our children. We don't have a lot of money, we can't get help. Diana needs to stay home and take responsibility for this baby."

Throughout this diatribe, Diana's stepfather, Don, sat quietly. He had heard it before. At this point in the session, the therapist thought the problem was primarily related to developmental and family life cycle challenges: Diana was very young when she had a child, out of phase for her culture, and she was unequipped developmentally to handle her new role. She did not adapt to this new reality in her life but rather maintained her preferred status as a carefree teenager. Her parents, for their part, also did not want to adapt. They felt they were through with child rearing and wanted a less hands-on, grandparent-like role rather than the primary parenting role they inherited.

This explanation was interesting but somehow seemed superficial. The therapist drew a genogram (see Figure 4.1) on easel paper with the family.

---

[1] All cases in this chapter are real but camouflaged to protect the family's identity. Some are amalgamations of families with similar problems, but their dynamics and outcomes are true to life.

Figure 4.1

Genogram of Diana's Family

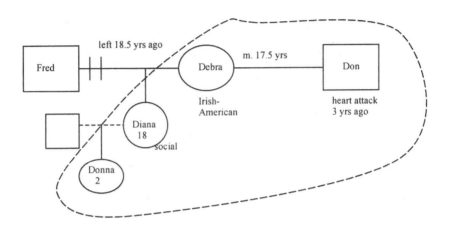

She asked Diana for the family history and learned that Diana's biological father left her mother while her mother was pregnant with her. When the therapist asked for her father's name, Diana said, "Bob," but her mother looked surprised and interrupted, "No, honey, it was Fred." Diana shrugged; she knew precious little about her biological father. He disappeared with the news of her mother's pregnancy. Her stepfather, Don, began dating her mother soon thereafter, and they married just after Diana's birth. Don was the only father Diana had ever known. As is typical, the therapist asked about Diana's grandparents and the significant health events in the family. Diana quickly said: "Well, my father [Don] had a heart attack several years ago."

The therapist said: "Really? Before you got pregnant?"

Diana: "Three months before."

As the family talked more about their history, it became clear that they associated pregnancy with loss (as when Fred left Debra) and that Don's heart attack had threatened both his wife and daughter with a new loss. Diana's pregnancy repeated this old theme, an intergenerational transmission of a pattern related to the potential loss of a father being associated with the birth of a baby. But this time, Don survived his heart attack, and Don and Debra wanted even more to enjoy their time together so that the baby became a source of struggle as well as joy.

Without taking a biopsychosocial family history, none of this information would have emerged. The meaning the family gave the pregnancy was not only about their "baby" having a baby but also carried the weight of these unresolved issues of loss related to Diana's biological father. There were many aspects to this therapy, but part of it had to do with Diana learning more about him and his relationship with her mother.

The "Patient" in Family Therapy

Any case can be understood from a family systems perspective, no matter how many people are in the therapist's office for help. Sometimes the referral is for one person, as with Diana who was labeled as the patient, and the family is both collaborator and participant in the treatment. Research on treatment for depressed individuals, for example, shows that couples counseling can be as or more effective for patients with depression (Beach, 2002), and psychoeducation for families of patients with schizophrenia or bipolar disorder can prevent or reduce relapse rates (Milkowitz & Goldstein, 1997). Sometimes the referral focuses on a relationship, such as with marital therapy, and the relationship becomes the "patient." In any case, the therapist completes a biopsychosocial evaluation, eliciting the individual, relationship, and social factors that contribute to the continuation of the problem, as occurred with Diana and her family. A systemic treatment plan, then, focuses on the level or levels of the system in which the therapist, patient, and family can get the most leverage for change.

Two Against One: Triangulation and Intergenerational Coalitions

Joey, age 10, was brought to therapy because he refused to go to school. Rick and Sally, his father and stepmother, begged and cajoled him every morning, sometimes plying his fingers off the bathroom towel railing and carrying him kicking and screaming to school. Joey often lasted at school about 2 hours; then the school staff called Sally, who worked from home, to pick him up because he was so disruptive. Without her husband at home and wanting to be a "good" rather than "evil" stepmother, Sally worked hard to calm Joey down with video games and homemade cookies. In truth, Sally thought Rick was too hard on his son, and occasionally she said so to Joey, feeling he had a right to know. Sally was also disappointed that Rick worked much longer hours after their marriage than before. Joey became her project, and they developed a warm relationship, except for the morning struggles over school. Sally did not see, until several sessions of therapy, how her warm behavior might result in Joey's desire to avoid the challenges of school. Rick, for his part, did not see that his distance and strict approach to parenting left him on the long side of the triangle, with his wife and son being closer, on the short sides. The treatment plan involved meetings with Rick and Sally to bring them closer and put them in charge, together, of Joey's behavior.

Intergenerational coalitions happen with some frequency in families who present for therapy. The longer and more entrenched they are, the more difficult the treatment. Treatment consists of detriangulation, of helping the parents, or parenting figures, to work out their differences so that no adult sides with a difficult child against the other adult. The child can then feel safe and secure in what is expected of him or her, and the parents can feel closer in their shared goal of successfully raising their child.

The Pursuer–Distancer Dance

Jorge, 42, and Maria, 33, met through a Puerto Rican Internet dating service and dated for 3 years. For most of that time, they organized their lives around Maria's genetic testing. She was becoming blind and losing her sense of balance. Jorge said he wanted to have a child with Maria, but only if the odds of repeating Maria's disorder were not high. "I'll take normal odds," he said. Maria was "eternally optimistic," constantly trying to persuade Jorge on their nightly phone calls that their child would be fine. The more Maria tried to convince him, the more Jorge wanted scientific proof.

Systems theory posits that human behavior is affected, even regulated, by those with whom we interact. Both Jorge and Maria had some worry or ambivalence about a pregnancy, but their interactions led them to polarize so that Jorge became the worrier and Maria the advocate (consistent with their temperaments) for their relationship. This dance, called pursuer and distancer in Bowen theory, is repeated over and over in therapists' offices (Fogarty, 1976). The family therapist creates space for the couple to speak about their concerns, verifying each position, and working to prevent polarization. Typically, the therapist works to help the pursuer see the pattern as it unfolds and "sit" with her anxiety, in the case of Maria, rather than pursuing her partner.

Therapist: Jorge, I can see how much you love Maria, and yet you are so concerned that you not enter into a partnership involving a child that you cannot handle.

Jorge: That's true [hanging his head]. I'm ashamed, but that's the way I feel.

Therapist: You want what's best for your future family.

Jorge: That's true. I don't want to worry all day about my wife and child.

Therapist: Jorge and Maria, I can see that you both are concerned about your future together and you both want what's best. Jorge, you tend to be the one expressing the worry, and Maria, the optimism, but these are issues you both should talk about. Maria, you don't want all the burden of responsibility to stay on Jorge's shoulders.

Maria: That's really true. I do think it will all be okay, but I think it's important to listen to the geneticists and address Jorge's concerns.

Therapist: It's so important to understand each other's hopes and fears, and be able to share them in a respectful way. I wonder if it would be useful to spend several weeks without talking about this issue, to try and clarify the many different aspects of the situation for each of you. When you do have a phone call, Maria, you express all the concern, and Jorge all the optimism. Just see how that feels, and what you learn from the exercise . . .

Maria agreed to not try and persuade Jorge during the 3 weeks before their next session. It was she who suggested this might be easiest if they didn't see each other during this time, an easier way for her to work toward individuation. Jorge started the next session by talking about how much he missed Maria and how he wanted their relationship to be long term. Frequently, when the pursuer pulls back, the distancer moves forward, as if there is a predictable (homeostatic) distance in a relationship that must be maintained. Rather than moving back into an old pattern, Maria was coached to continue her focus on her own functioning, while Jorge was encouraged to take more time to consider this important decision. Many couples must sustain a different pattern of behavior for some time before it becomes a new and healthier homeostasis.

Collaboration and the Role of the Larger System

Many patients have more people than just their families involved with their problems: they have schools, social service agencies, attorneys, doctors, and other health professionals. The possibilities are limitless. The goal of the family therapist is to determine the players who have a major effect on the problem and whether those people need to be involved in the treatment.

In the situation with Jorge and Maria, the geneticist was a major player. With the couple's permission, it was important for the therapist to communicate with him.

Therapist: Dr. Reed, thank you for referring Maria and Jorge. They sure are concerned about the possibility of passing on Maria's disorder to a future child.

Dr. Reed: I know. They seem to want certainty that I can't provide.

Therapist: Jorge keeps talking about odds. I know you geneticists think in terms of risk. I wonder if you could speak to them in terms of odds. This seems to be the language with which Jorge discusses the problem.

Dr. Reed: I appreciate that suggestion. Certainly it is not working to offer them one more genetic test that is highly unlikely to be positive. Let me review the data and see what I might offer them in the way of an explanation in terms they'll understand.

The next therapy session occurred right after their meeting with the geneticist. Jorge was elated: "He told us we are likely to have no greater than normal odds of having a baby with Maria's disorder. In fact, he said we'd be more likely to have a baby with cystic fibrosis . . . and amniocentesis can test for that!" Maria just smiled. After the session, the therapist e-mailed her geneticist collaborator, telling him the couple seemed to be doing very well with the news. Dr. Reed wrote back: "I gave them the same talk over and over, and could see it was not being helpful. Once you got involved, I decided to try something different. I'm glad that we succeeded." Sometimes making a change in one part of the system will create a reverberating change in another. Though it was not planned as such, the family therapist's approach to this couple helped the geneticist to see them and then treat them differently.

FAMILY THERAPIST–PATIENT RELATIONSHIPS

In family therapy, the relationship between family members is primary, not the relationship between the therapist and the patient or family. In psychoanalysis or psychodynamic psychotherapy, the transference of the patient's introject of a parental figure onto the therapist becomes the grist for interpretation and exploration. In family therapy, it is the *actual* relationships that are the focus of treatment. Behavior therapists may talk with patients about how significant others reward progress or unwittingly reinforce symptoms. In family therapy, those positive and negative reinforcements are available for view in the therapy room directly. Because of this, the intimacy in the room is typically between family members rather than with the therapist.

Part of the challenge for the family therapist is developing what Ivan Boszormenyi-Nagy (1973) termed *multilateral partiality*, or alliances with all members of the family. This term refers to the need for the family therapist to form strong relationships of trust and fairness with each member of the family, without taking sides and inadvertently forming a coalition with one member of the family against another (a professional version of an intergenerational coalition). This can be difficult when, for example, an adolescent is appealing and a parent appears to be too harsh. However, forming a warm bond with the adolescent while remaining cool with the parent only inflames the problem. Instead, the therapist is charged with finding something in each family member to connect with, recognizing that this kind of neutrality (or better said, multipartial alliance) is part of the healing aspects of most family therapy.[2] With multiple patients, there are inevitably multiple agendas. In the case of Jorge and Maria, the therapist worked to understand both party's positions—Jorge's worrying and Maria's advocacy for the relationship. By describing both positions respectfully, the therapist joined successfully with both members of the couple without siding with one against the other.

The Role of the Therapist

The family therapist is in charge of the structure of treatment (Whitaker & Bumberry, 1988). This means that the therapist will organize the timing of the sessions, where and how they will occur, and who should come. He or she may suggest homework assignments to diagnose the problem and test the family's willingness to change.

The family therapist is also in charge of the communication in therapy. With more than one person, and sometimes many people, in the room, the therapist has many relationships to develop and manage. He or she becomes a kind of traffic cop—teaching family members to communicate without blame, listen respectfully to each other, acknowledge they heard what was said, and learn to deal with conflict, difference, and emotional intensity. The therapist wants to hear the individual and family stories, to understand their belief systems, and, like an applied anthropologist, to help the family find the solutions to their pain and their problems from within their culture and value systems.

The therapist may also be something of a teacher, educating or showing patients how their behavior affects each other. A common example of this is when a depressed patient is demanding and difficult when he feels badly so that his spouse distances from him, which only leads the patient to feel more depressed and be more difficult. Uncovering these cycles, or cycles related to violence or child misbehavior or psychosomatic illness, all can be foci of family therapy, helping the family to recognize the effect of each individual's behavior on the other.

---

[2] This does not mean condoning abusive behavior. Families with disorders of power, such as partner violence or sexual abuse, need clear, external limits on destructive behavior. However, all therapists are most effective when they can connect and form a trusting relationship with each member of a family.

The Role of the Patient and Family

While the therapist is in charge of the treatment, the family is in charge of the initiative for change (Whitaker, 1988). It is critical that the therapist not become more invested and motivated in change than the family. Otherwise, a pursuer–distancer dynamic occurs with the therapist as pursuer, often resulting in the family backing away from change (Fogarty, 1976). The skill of the therapist is in increasing the patient and family's motivation for change.

Sandra and Molly came to therapy because of some mild partner violence (Sandra had slapped Molly on the arm once); both said they wanted to stop this destructive way of relating before it got worse. When the therapist tried to schedule an intake session, neither member of the couple could agree on when to come in. Finally, both said that Wednesday at 8 p.m. would work, though the therapist had stated that she only saw patients until 7 p.m. The therapist was tempted to bend the commitment to herself and her own family out of concern for this couple's problem. However, recognizing a potentially unhelpful pattern at the beginning of therapy, she said she would work hard to schedule them, but it had to be some time during her regular office hours before 7 p.m. Whitaker & Bumberry (1988) called this the "battle for structure," and insisted the therapist must win this battle for treatment to succeed.

The therapist also asked Sandra and Molly each to take notes any time either of them began to feel angry and bring the notes into therapy, thereby working to increase their motivation for change. Whitaker called this the "battle for initiative," and insisted that the family must win this battle for treatment to succeed.

BRIEF AND LONG-TERM STRATEGIES AND TECHNIQUES

The techniques and strategies of family therapy operationalize systems thinking and can be used in single-session therapy or long-term work. Goal setting, in the beginning, allows the family and the therapist to stay focused and measure the progress and outcome of therapy. The use of tools such as the genogram, time lines, and sculpting organize complex family information so that it is useful to the family and the therapist. Techniques such as positive connotation and listing family strengths help to broaden the assessment of the presenting problem. Circular questions, enactment, and externalizing the problem are techniques that put the presenting complaint in context.

Goal Setting

Family therapy is an active therapy. Early in treatment, the therapist works to define the presenting problem, the people involved with the problem, the interpersonal patterns of behavior related to the problem, and the criteria by which each family member would know if the therapy is successful. Goal setting becomes a group activity, with the therapist working to help the family negotiate common achievable goals in their own words. This is not so easy. (If it were, the family would likely not need therapy!) Sometimes, goal setting can take several sessions because family members do not agree on the definition of the problem or the desired outcome. Also, many times initial goals are framed in unachievable terms.

Sonia, for example, stated that her goal for couples therapy was to have her husband, Reynolds, never express anger with her. Therapy then focused on psychoeducational principles that normalize anger so an appropriate goal focused instead on *how* Sonia wishes Reynolds to express his anger to her.

Enactment

In many psychotherapies, patients talk *about* other relationships and problems. In family therapy, these relationships and problems are brought into the room. After setting a goal about dealing with anger, the therapist asked Reynolds to show how he acts when he's angry with Sonia. "Assume that you had a bad day at work. Then think of something that Sonia does that is sometimes irritating. Turn to her and show me what happens when you're angry."

The in-session enactment allows the therapist and the patients to witness the problem firsthand. The patients can then reflect on the experience, and the therapist can coach them on alternative ways of communicating. "Try telling Sonia when you come in the door: 'Honey, I had a stressful day at work. Let me tell you about it.' Monitor your own internal experience to make sure that you don't take out your difficult day on the person you love the most." After the couple tried out this new way of communicating, the therapist advised, "When expressing your feelings about an irritating habit, be sure to start with: 'When you leave your work-out clothes on the floor, it makes me angry. I feel like you want me to do all the cleaning up in the house, even though we both have outside jobs.'"

Circular Questions

Family therapists use interview techniques that reveal the nature of relationships in the family (Selvini-Palazzoli et al., 1980). One of those techniques, called circular questions, sometimes brings to light longstanding misunderstandings.

Therapist: Sonia, when Reynolds leaves his clothes on the floor, what is he trying to communicate to you?

Sonia: He wants me to become a better housewife. He's hoping I'll do his chores as part of that. But I'm not!

Reynolds: [looking shocked] This is not a test of your skills! I've always been sloppy in the bedroom. I need to change that now that I have a roommate.

Externalizing the Problem

A family therapy technique introduced by Michael White (White & Epston, 1990) moves the problem outside of one individual or one relationship. Externalizing the problem reduces blaming behavior that can prevent the problem from being resolved.

Bill and Stella came for therapy because Stella was having recurrent spells of blanking out. At first her physician thought she might have epilepsy, but long-term monitoring in the hospital revealed that these spells were psychogenic in origin. The neurologist thought their timing was related to marital stress and referred the couple for therapy. In the second session, after setting goals that included reducing the blanking out spells and improving their marriage, the therapist asked Stella and Bill to consider these spells as something external to both of them.

"What do the spells look like?" the therapist asked. "What color are they? Do they have a name? Are they like an animal, a plant, a person?"

Stella and Bill had surprisingly little disagreement about the nature of the spells. Stella said they were red, "hot like a fire." Bill agreed, adding they were "like a red porcupine, all sharp and bristly." These descriptions gave the therapist valuable information about the possible relationship of these spells to anger in the relationship. When she asked about a name for this porcupine, Stella said, "Porky."

To some extent this exercise served to desensitize both members of the couple to talking about the spells, which had heretofore been mysterious and somewhat scary. The therapist then set about to find out when Porky was likely to come on the scene and to slowly help the couple learn to identify their anger and express it appropriately. Two sessions after externalizing this symptom, Stella revealed that Bill was sometimes emotionally abusive to her. Her Catholic faith, she felt, did not permit her to express anger back. She now noticed that Porky tended to appear in reaction to Bill's emotional tirades. Over time, Bill was placed on antidepressants as an aid to learning self-regulation skills. As his verbal abuse eased, Stella's blanking spells stopped altogether. Both continued to work on communication and anger management.

Family Sculpting

Another technique that serves as both assessment and intervention is that of family sculpting (Satir, 1988). Most commonly, the therapist asks one family member to place other family members in a physical pose, as if in a sculpture, to represent the way that sculptor views the family functioning. The therapist may ask for three sculpts: one from an important time in the past, one in the present, and one that shows how the family member would like to see the family functioning in the future. This exercise is often more revealing than verbal description. Each family member may get a chance, so that differing perspectives (e.g., from a married couple) may be illuminated and discussed.

For example, when asked to sculpt how the couple's relationships is at present, Stella set herself in one corner working and her husband Bill in another. Bill's sculpt was similar, except he was playing racquetball while Stella was at home reading. When asked how she wanted it to be, Stella sat herself and Bill side by side, very still, each staring lovingly at their interlocking hands. For his part, Bill walked the couple around a garden pointing out interesting plants and flowers. This exercise revealed the couple's differing temperaments and goals for the relationship much more vividly than their earlier verbal descriptions.

Positively Connoting the Resistance to Change

In individual psychotherapy, the therapist works to understand what stands in the way of a patient resolving a problem. In family therapy, this same process becomes an interactional exercise as the therapist positively connotes the resistance. This positive connotation allows the patient and family to advocate for change.

With Stella and Bill, for example, the therapist posited that Stella must have good reasons for blanking out, perhaps things she didn't want to hear or say to Bill, given their long-term love and devotion to each other. This comment led to Stella watching for her own anger just before blanking out. With Bill, the therapist commented that he must recognize the importance of expressing negative feelings in a relationship. Perhaps his feelings were so intense because he was expressing them for both members of the couple. If Stella were able to begin to express her own irritations or anger, perhaps Bill could take responsibility for expressing his in a more appropriate way. Positively connoting Bill's behavior allowed him to take charge of his anger without inducing shame that would only result in more symptoms.

Genograms and Time Lines

Genograms and time lines are invaluable tools for the family therapist to organize the complicated data about a family's history and relationships. These tools are often interventions in and of themselves. Posting them on easel paper allows the family to see holes in their information (such as when Diana didn't know her biological father's name) and patterns across generations ("I never realized how many divorces there are in my family until we put it up on the board like this"). Time lines allow families to associate important events, such as job loss, illness, or death, with the development of symptoms.

Sandy and Sean came to therapy because of Sandy's loss of sexual desire. In the second session, the therapist suggested they draw a time line beginning with when they met, including all the important events from that time forward. Both members of the couple realized that Sandy's sexual desire waned after the birth of their third child, which occurred soon after the death of her mother. This association allowed for a focus on unresolved grief before returning to strengthening the couple's intimacy, both verbally and physically. Genograms and time lines also reduce the blaming that can occur in families when intimacy fails.

Building on Family Strengths

Systemic family therapy focuses on individual and family strengths as a way to resolve symptoms or problems. It assumes that amplifying positive behaviors often works much better than careful attention to pathology. This means that goals are always framed in positive terms (what the family wants more, rather than less, of). Gathering information for a genogram always includes asking about individual and family strengths. For example:

- What did you learn from your grandmother?
- Even with all his faults, what positive life lessons did you learn from your father?
- What would you say are the strengths in your family? What have you learned from them that has helped you in life?
- What do you want to make sure to pass down to your children?

The miracle question, introduced in chapter 2 in the discussion of solution-focused therapy, is also an example of a strength-based approach. For example: "If you could go to sleep tonight and wake up tomorrow with all your problems solved, what specifically would that look like? What would be you doing? What would your spouse be doing? What would your children be doing? And, what are the first steps to take in moving from here to there?"

In-Depth Case Example

Greta and John are an African American couple in their late 40s who presented for therapy because John had secretly overspent their savings in the past several years so the family was on the verge of bankruptcy. Greta was outraged, and John felt crushed and exposed in his inability to support his family.

As is frequently the case, this couple's problems began during a point of stress in the family life cycle. Greta had turned the bills and finances over to John when their triplets were 10, feeling overwhelmed with the tasks of running the household and caring for the children. In the first session, a genogram revealed that Greta came from an upper-middle-class family. Her father was an attorney and her mother a CPA (see Figure 4.2). The family was active in church, and her parents were community leaders. John's family was lower-middle class. His father worked in a manufacturing plant and was laid off at age 55. While never feeling "poor," John said his family struggled to make ends meet. The therapist wondered about how these different family cultures, and the meaning that money had for them, may have influenced the development of this couple's problems.

In the second and third sessions, the therapist asked Greta and John to give a history of their marriage, starting with their first date. For most couples, this exercise brings back fond memories and underscores their attraction, commonalities, and commitment to each other. Watching Greta and John, it was clear that they shared many common values about their children, their family, and their commitment to community. In fact, both said they rarely had disagreements until this blowup. This comment led to an exploration about how each family handled anger (Greta's family never expressed anger while John's family did so in an abusive way) and how the couple's similar values and differing training in their families of origin resulted in them never learning how to effectively express anger or resolve disagreements. They had an enmeshed relationship in which one of the family rules was to never express anger, but it came out in other ways. Both agreed this was true, with John's overspending being the most egregious example. The therapist said that while this problem hurt Greta's trust in John and caused much pain and suffering, it was a problem they

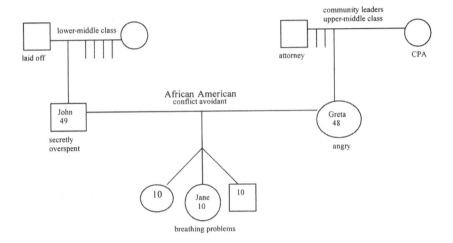

Figure 4.2

Genogram of Greta and John's Family

could resolve. In a sense, John "chose" a relatively solvable problem to bring them into therapy to learn the skills that had been avoided to date.

John was the identified patient for a problem that was multifaceted and shared by both members of the couple. For example, John dated the problem to when Greta pulled away from him to care for the triplets. Both shared the view that they must be proud and hide any problems because of the prejudice they had experienced from the larger community.

At the end of the third session, the couple decided to turn all finances back to Greta until she decided she trusted John again. Then they might decide to do the finances together, understanding now that it is a vulnerable point in their relationship. Until that time, they agreed to meet once a week for Greta to go over the finances so that John remained informed, though he had no decision-making power. This plan focused on the finances (moving them out of the danger zone) and trust (dealing with what Greta felt was a betrayal). However, a more comprehensive treatment plan was needed to deal with the underpinnings of this problem, including improving the couple's communication and increasing their individual and dyadic ability to tolerate and express negative affect and differences of opinion (differentiation). The couple then focused on using these skills to increase their intimacy and problem-solving abilities as well as their effectiveness in parenting.

The fourth session focused on communication skills, especially with regard to anger. Both Greta and John so avoided talking about negative feelings that the session mostly consisted of psychoeducation by the therapist, with a plan for the next session to involve telling each other directly how each felt about the current situation. Before they could finish, Greta said one of their daughters, Jane, had developed "breathing problems" (a clear example of a biopsychosocial problem and the intergenerational transmission of anxiety). Jane was having what Greta thought was mild asthma at night, and she seemed anxious during the day. Greta, starting to understand how relationships affect behavior, asked: "Do you think this could be related to our problems? We haven't told the children anything about our problems." The therapist suggested taking their daughter to the pediatrician to evaluate her breathing problem. (It is always important to have somatic problems evaluated medically.) She also said the emotional climate at home certainly affected the children, and the more they can improve their marriage, the more healthy the home for the children.

In two weeks, both members of the couple arrived for their "anger session," as they called it, looking red and shaky. John said he had been up most of the night worrying. With some coaching by the therapist, Greta started by telling John how she felt about him driving the family into debt. It was hard for her to articulate her anger. John perspired while Greta struggled to be straight. The therapist coached them on good communication skills, including repeating what they heard, not interrupting, and using "I" statements. With great difficulty, Greta was able to tell John how angry she was and why. John was able to hear her anger, accept it, and express some of his loneliness and desire for greater intimacy. At the end of the session, both said they were relieved and felt that they could expand on the session at home. The therapist suggested that each individual keep a journal tracking her or his emotions and deciding which of these to communicate to her or his partner. The next several sessions were spent continuing to improve communication, normalize feelings, and increase intimacy. In the eighth session, Greta remarked that their daughter was much less anxious and not having significant breathing problems anymore. (The same could be said for her parents!) The couple came to therapy for six more sessions, wanting to make sure they were building a more solid foundation of trust, communication, and problem-solving skills. The therapy ended with an invitation to return at any point for a checkup or a booster session. If they decided not to return, the therapist requested a note updating her on their progress.

OBSTACLES AND CHALLENGES OF A FAMILY SYSTEMS APPROACH

Each of the challenges of this approach also reveals its strengths. Probably the biggest challenge is that Western culture is embedded in a highly individualistic, reductionistic culture. People's strengths and problems are viewed as belonging to them, individually. They are not understood as influenced by relationships or context. Our individualistic culture means that many patients do not immediately see the connection between their behavior and the problem. At the same time, this challenge is also one of the theory's most valuable assets. In essence, it corrects for our culture's overfocus on the individual and encourages people to be more responsible toward those they love.

Deriving from this same problem, sometimes it is difficult to succeed at getting patients to bring their family members into therapy. It may take extra effort, for example, to bring a father into the treatment of his daughter with eating disorders. In his mind, it is his daughter's problem, and his wife may be best suited to attend the meetings regarding the problem. Fortunately, most family members will eventually agree to come once: The patient believes that the therapist will treat family members with respect and not blame them for problems; family members believe their views will be of help to the patient and they themselves won't be blamed; and the family members believe the therapist will be balanced in his or her approach and support individuals and their relationships with each other.

Another of the challenges is the complexity of systems theory and family therapy. Conducting a family interview with angry or anxious family members takes considerable skill and considerable time to learn those skills. Training often includes "live" supervision, so that a supervisor or group can observe a session and provide immediate feedback to the therapist. Video is also often helpful, in order to gather the relevant data that is impossible for one person to absorb in a fast-paced session with multiple people.

Family therapists work at multiple levels—the biological, the individual, the couple, the family, the larger system, and the culture. They assess the problem at all these levels and then make a judgment about where one may get the most leverage for change. While the complexity is a challenge, it provides an accurate representation of the human experience. Family therapy has depth and meaning and focuses people on improving relationships with the people about whom they care the most.

5

Evaluation

Family therapy was founded by a generation of therapists with a bold new idea about the causes of mental illness and a set of innovative intervention tools. These pioneers saw themselves as researchers into the mysteries of family communication. Schizophrenia in families sparked their interest more than anything else. The Palo Alto team studied communication in families of hospitalized patients. Bowen brought families into apartment-like settings to observe their everyday behavior. Wynne examined disordered communication patterns of families with a member with schizophrenia. When it came to treatment, however, most of the founders saw the effectiveness of their therapy models as self-evident: They were brilliant clinicians, and families were changing in therapy, and besides, there was little empirical tradition at the time for evaluating the effectiveness of any form of psychotherapy. It was not until the second and third generations of family therapy that studies began to systematically evaluate the effects of family therapy.

Two major challenges facing family therapy effectiveness researchers were the relatively global nature of family systems theory and the lack of specificity of many of the intervention techniques. If you contrast the family theories and therapy approaches you've read about in this book with, say, behavioral theories and therapies, you can readily see the challenge. Assessing and treating family enmeshment is a long cry from assessing and treating agoraphobia.

But by the late 1970s strong calls began to appear for the field to prove its worth as a treatment modality. Gurman and Kniskern (1981) were among the first to pull together the limited body of efficacy research and call for more empirical evidence to support family therapy. Around this time the field began a tidal shift away from nonacademic training institutes toward university-based academic programs in psychology and marriage and family therapy. The path was then open to the emergence of family therapy evaluation research.

In a nutshell, after nearly three decades of research we know that family therapy is effective for a wide range of behavioral and mental health disorders. In their comprehensive overview of meta-analyses of family therapy outcome studies, Shadish and Baldwin (2002) reported that family therapy consistently produces positive change greater than no-treatment control groups across a variety of problem areas. As with studies of individual psychotherapy, there is little evidence that one form of family therapy is consistently superior to another. (Indeed, most of the evidence-based family therapies described in this chapter are deliberately integrative of several models of family therapy.) When family therapy is compared to individual adult psychotherapy, few overall differences are found—with the prominent exception of treatment for alcoholism. However, in several areas of childhood, adolescent, and young adult therapy, family therapy outperforms individual therapy. These areas include childhood oppositional defiant and conduct disorder, adolescent eating disorders, and schizophrenia among young adults. The bulk of this chapter will cover major areas of family therapy outcome research. We will also discuss what research has to say about family therapy with diverse patient populations.

MAJOR AREAS OF FAMILY THERAPY OUTCOME RESEARCH

Family therapy research has primarily focused on those issues for which family therapy has proven more effective than other forms of psychotherapy. As mentioned previously, these issues range from schizophrenia to childhood disorders, to alcohol and substance abuse. This section provides a sample of this research.

Family Psychoeducation for Schizophrenia

As we mentioned previously, family therapy began with hopes for a psychosocial cure for schizophrenia and ran into the intractability of an illness with a strong biological base. Over time, however, the bloom went off the biological-only approach as patients recycled in and out of hospitals following repeated psychotic breaks over the years. The expressed emotion research described in chapter 2 pointed to a promising new approach to treatment that combined medication with a family treatment for reducing negative family interactions. This new approach, termed family psychoeducation, differed in an important way from traditional family therapy in not assuming that family dynamics caused the illness; rather, the family has a role in whether the illness is controlled or the patient has repeated relapses (Anderson, 1983).

There are several forms of family psychoeducational treatment for schizophrenia, including individual family treatment and treatment with groups of families. Patients are generally young adults with schizophrenia or schizoaffective disorders who have experienced a psychotic episode and a hospitalization. The treatment involves a didactic component and a family change component. Families are taught that schizophrenia is a brain disease caused by a variety of factors, some known and some not yet known. It runs in families—that is, it has a genetic component—but family problems do not cause the disease. Once the illness occurs, however, certain psychosocial stresses in the family create risk for relapse, and families can take steps to improve their communication and problem-solving capacities to help prevent relapse. This involves learning to be supportive but not intrusive, to reduce everyday levels of intensity, to avoid heated conflict, and to engage in constructive problem solving. This approach to working with the family (adapted by Anderson, 1983, from structural family therapy) is accompanied by other vocational and rehabilitation services, with the family heavily involved in helping their ill member to become engaged with the community.

In a large number of studies comparing family psychoeducation plus medical management to medical management plus standard supportive counseling for the patient, family psychoeducation has proved to be highly effective in preventing relapse and rehospitalization. Twenty-seven studies reviewed by McFarlane, Dixon, Lukens, and Luksted (2003) found positive results, while only three studies did not. The family psychoeducation treatment groups averaged 50% lower rates of rehospitalization. In recent years, with this finding so well established, researchers have shifted their focus to additional aspects of the illness, particularly its effects on everyday life and participation in community. Results have been positive in these areas as well, with increased patient participation in vocational rehabilitation, higher employment rates, and improved social functioning as a result of family psychoeducation and community support (MacFarlane et al., 2003).

It is ironic that the powerful effects of family therapy have been found for a disorder that the field largely walked away from after the first generation. Giving up on a full explanation of the origins of schizophrenia led the second generation of family therapists to reenter the field of schizophrenia treatment with more humility and produce remarkable results. Unfortunately, however, this evidence-based approach to treating schizophrenia has not yet widely penetrated a treatment field committed in an individual, biomedical approach. Dissemination is a central focus of current efforts by leaders in this important area of work. In the meantime, researchers are also replicating the positives effects of family psychoeducation with schizophrenia with another serious biologically based mental illness—bipolar disorder—where individual treatments outside of psychopharmacological ones have not been especially effective (Rea et al., 2003).

Adolescent Conduct Disorders

Three family therapy models have proven effective in treating adolescent conduct disorders—functional family therapy, multisystemic therapy, and the Treatment Foster Care Program of the Oregon Social Learning Center (Chamberlain & Reid, 1998). Studies in this area have been exemplary in terms of rigorous, "gold standard" criteria laid out by scholars such as Kazdin and Weisz (1998): (a) multiple randomized clinical trials; (b) well-described, replicable treatment procedures; (c) uniform training of therapists and careful monitoring of their fidelity to the treatment model; (d) use of real-world, clinical samples; (e) broad-based assessment of outcomes; and (f) evidence of long-term outcomes.

To single out the model with the most evidence, multisystemic therapy, created by Henggeler and his colleagues, is a home-based approach that works closely with schools and other community systems (Henggeler, Schoenwald, Borduin, Rowland, & Cunningham, 1998). Treatment is intensive, involving about 60 hours of direct service over 3 to 6 months. Therapists have small caseloads and are on call to families 24 hours a day, 7 days per week. The clinical procedures in multisystem therapy (MST) are derived from strategic family therapy, structural family therapy, behavior parent training, cognitive–behavioral therapies, and ecosystemic therapies. Psychopharmacological interventions are also incorporated as needed. When parents and other family caregivers have problems that interfere with treatment goals for the adolescent, the therapist helps them get treatment for their problems.

The typical outcome study of MST involves youth presenting with serious antisocial behavior and at acute risk of out-of-home placement. Reduction rates for recidivism have ranged between 25% and 70% across studies in comparison with control groups receiving standard care. MST has produced decreased out-of-home placement days by 47% to 64% compared to usual services, and these differences have held up to 5 years of follow-up (Henggeler & Sheidow, 2002). MST has been demonstrated to be a highly effective way to treat adolescent conduct disorder.

Adolescent Substance Abuse

In their review of family therapy outcomes in adolescent drug abuse, Rowe and Liddle (2003) found family therapy superior to any other intervention. The major models of family therapy shown to be effective are multisystemic therapy, multidimensional family therapy, and functional family therapy. All of these models work intensively with the family and with community systems.

Multidimensional family therapy (MDFT) for adolescent drug abuse was created by Howard Liddle and his colleagues (Liddle et al., 2001) out of structural and strategic family therapy models. MDFT has three phases consisting of individual and family sessions. The first phase builds therapeutic alliances with the adolescent, parents/family, and important stakeholders outside the family. Here goals are set and agreed upon. The second phase helps the adolescent to build skills in handling stress and communicating with others, the parents to develop better skills in relating to the adolescent, and the whole family to learn better ways of dealing with challenges in their relationships. The third phase helps the family learn how to relate to the outside world and to plan for their family life after the therapy ends.

Functional family therapy was developed by James Alexander in the 1970s as a way to treat oppositional children and adolescents and became one of the first evidence-based models in the field (Sexton & Alexander, 2002). Originally a behaviorist, Alexander incorporated strategic family therapy and other models into an integrative approach that starts from the assumption that negative child and adolescent behaviors serve functions within the family, such as attempts to become more connected. Functional family therapists aim to help the family achieve its goals through more constructive means rather than symptomatic means. Reframing the child's negative behavior as a misguided attempt to do something good for the family is one of the distinctive therapeutic tools in this model. The three phases of treatment are: engagement and motivation, behavior change, and generalization.

In comparison with standard treatments, MDFT, functional family therapy, and MST have been found superior in the following areas summarized by Rowe and Liddle (2003):

- Engagement and retention in treatment. These models all have strong family engagement protocols that get resistant adolescents into therapy and keep them in therapy.
- Effects on drug use. Family therapy decreases the use of a variety of drugs, including alcohol, marijuana, cocaine, and heroin. These effects tend to be long term.
- Related emotional and behavior problems. The multiple system focus is effective at reducing non-drug behavioral problems, especially exter-

nalizing problems. Adolescents who have had family therapy improve their school outcomes as well.

- Family functioning. Families improve on areas such as cohesion and conflict more than in other therapies.
- Cost effectiveness. Initial studies indicate that family therapy is more cost effective than standard treatment programs.

Childhood Behavioral and Emotional Disorders

These disorders cover a wide spectrum, with evidence for family therapy's effectiveness strong for some problems, moderate for others, and scant for some.

The strongest evidence is for oppositional defiant disorder, where the Oregon Social Learning Center's parent training (PT) model is one of the best validated treatments in the whole field of psychotherapy. PT came out of the observational research of Gerald Patterson (1971) and his colleagues on problematic family interaction patterns of kids with oppositional defiant disorder. These include coercive behaviors (yelling, physical aggression, focus on disapproval statements, and negative commands) and other forms of poor parenting (such as ineffective consequences and low rates of positive attention). Parents and children get into negative, escalating, reinforcing chains of coercive interaction.

PT works with parents to teach them to shape more constructive child behavior by setting a goal and reinforcing the child's successive approximations toward that goal. To manage escalating behavioral interactions, parents are taught a variety of techniques, including time-outs (generally 5 minutes) to isolate the child until the outburst subsides. If children resist the time-out, minutes are added and then a privilege taken away. Children generally learn to cooperate rather than lose privileges. Parents are also taught how to monitor their children's outside relationships and to make effective requests (short and simple).

Over a wide range of studies, PT has been found effective in diminishing childhood behavioral and emotional disorders. As summarized by Northey, Wells, Silverman, and Bailey (2003): "Parent Training for oppositional behavior problems on children is one of the most well-researched treatment modalities in child psychology and there is incontrovertible evidence for its short-term effectiveness, especially with younger opposition behavior problem children (i.e., ages 6 to 12 years)" (p. 103). There is also increasing evidence that PT is effective in treating attention deficit/hyperactivity disorder (ADHD) in particular. There is more limited research on family therapy for "internalizing" problems in children, especially anxiety and depression, and no conclusions can be drawn except that results seem to be comparable to individual therapy (Northey et al., 2003).

Anorexia Nervosa in Adolescence

Anorexia nervosa has confounded individual treatment approaches. Outcomes for standard treatment are not optimistic. Across studies, only 44% of patients followed at least 4 years after the onset of illness are considered recovered—that is, being within 15% of ideal body weight—while one-quarter of patients remain seriously ill, and another 5% have succumbed to the illness and died. Rates of death for adults with chronic anorexia nervosa are even higher (Le Grange & Lock, 2007).

The extraordinarily creative team at the Philadelphia Child Guidance Clinic led by Salvador Minuchin was the first to tackle family therapy for anorexia nervosa (Minuchin et al., 1978), an intractable disorder with few successful psychosocial treatment options. Although not a systematic evaluation study, this work stimulated the development of other models, the best evaluated one being the Maudsley family treatment model developed in London from a structural family therapy base (Le Grange, Binford, & Loeb, 2005). The Maudsley model was developed for adolescents who are living with their families. It is a relatively short-term model (often 20 sessions over 6 months) in which the therapist intervenes assertively in the first stages of illness. Unlike standard approaches where parents are given general and mild advice about how to manage their child's eating, the Maudsley approach puts the parents directly in charge of getting their daughter or son to eat. The parents assert their hierarchical authority to insist that the adolescent eat responsibly and healthily. The whole family is encouraged to "externalize" the anorexia by viewing it as something that takes over or tricks the adolescent rather than being a part of the adolescent's personality.

Echoing psychoeducational models for schizophrenia, the Maudsley approach does not view parents as causes of the eating disorder. Rather parents are encouraged to use their creative resources to move their child toward health by feeding their child the type and amounts of food needed to restore health. After ideal body weight has been restored and other indicators of health are on track, the adolescent regains responsibility for self-feeding. In later stages of therapy, the therapist turns to issues of normal adolescent development by supporting the adolescent's autonomy, establishing appropriate parent–child boundaries, and helping parents with their own individual and marital needs as appropriate.

The Maudsley model has been found effective in numerous clinical trials (Le Grange et al., 2005). Over a variety of studies, 70% of patients reach a healthy weight by the end of treatment, while a majority of girls have started or resumed menstruation. At 5 years post-treatment, 75 to 90% of patients are fully recovered and no more than 10 to 15% remain seriously ill. These results are best for younger adolescents and for those whose illness have not yet become chronic. This model of family therapy has found its way into an increasing number of treatment facilities in the United States after the publication of a user-friendly treatment manual (Locke et al., 2002).

Alcohol Abuse in Adults

In the mid-1970s the U.S. National Institute on Alcohol Abuse and Alcoholism made a case for outcome studies family therapy, which the agency declared as a highly promising area of therapy for adult alcohol problems. Indeed, there were already a number of clinical innovations using marital and family therapy, but few empirical studies of their effects. That situation no longer holds: There are now a large number of well-designed studies.

The most heavily researched approach is behavioral couples therapy (BCT), which was developed in the 1970s to apply social learning theory and behavioral theory to couple relationships, with an emphasis on communication training and behavioral contracting to increase positive interactions and reduce negative ones (Jacobson & Margolin, 1979). As applied to alcohol problems, BCT aims to build support for abstinence and improve relationship quality and functioning among married or cohabiting people dealing with alcoholism. In addition to standard BCT techniques, the treatment of alcoholism involves a daily "sobriety contract" in which the alcoholic restates his or her intention to not drink and the spouse/partner reiterates support for this effort (O'Farrell, 1989). If the alcoholic is taking a medication such as disulfiram, the medication is taken with the spouse witnessing and verbally reinforcing (O'Farrell & Bayog, 1986). Research has shown that BCT yields more abstinence and better relationship functioning than standard individually based treatments. It also reduces domestic violence and emotional problems in the couple's children (O'Farrell & Fals-Stewart, 1999).

In addition to BCT, there is evidence that family systems therapies (strategic family therapy and related models) are effective in reducing drinking and promoting better family functioning (O'Farrell & Fals-Stewart, 1999). Furthermore, family therapy has been shown effective in motivating people to enter treatment, a major issue in the whole field of substance abuse treatment (Edwards & Steinglass, 1995; Stanton, 2004). In general, over the nearly 4 decades since the federal government noted the promise of family therapy and called for research on its effectiveness, the evidence is now clear that family therapy approaches, when adapted carefully, can be more effective than individual approaches to treating alcoholism in adults.

Interventions With Physical Disorders

An increasingly fertile area for family therapy is psychosocial treatment of physical disorders, particularly chronic medical conditions where traditional biomedical approaches have not been adequate (McDaniel et al., 1992). Research has demonstrated the powerful effect of family relationships on physical health and medical risk factors (Berkman, 2000). This influence occurs through the quality of family relationships affecting stress and physical well-being and also through how families support or undermine individuals' efforts to manage their own health practices.

Family protective factors found in the research literature include family closeness, caregiver coping skills, mutually supportive relationships, clear family organization, and direct communication about the illness. Family risk factors include conflict or criticism, external stressors, family isolation, and rigidity (Weihs, Fisher, & Baird, 2002).

With this research in mind, and with the entry of family therapists into medical environments, behavioral scientists have been documenting the effect of family interventions on a variety of physical disorders. These interventions range in intensity from family support groups to psychoeducational groups to individual family therapy (Campbell, 2003). Outcomes include health behaviors, such as adherence to medical regimens and smoking cessation and biological markers such as blood sugar control and blood pressure regulation.

This area of family therapy research is still in its infancy (Campbell, 2002) but has shown consistent positive results in a few areas. The most prominent area has been the health and functioning of people with dementia (Mittelman, Ferris, Shulman, Steinberg, & Levin, 1996). There is also promising research on the effectiveness of family interventions on some children's disorders such as asthma (Panton & Barley, 2002) and diabetes mellitus (Campbell, 2002).

DOES FAMILY THERAPY WORK WITH DIVERSE POPULATIONS?

Much more work is needed to evaluate the effectiveness of family therapy with diverse populations. Because of early work by Minuchin, Haley, and others with low-income, ethnic minority populations, the field has reason to be optimistic that its methods are not confined to the traditional therapy population of white, educated, middle-class people. Of special note is that recent evidence-based models (MST, MDFT) for child and adolescent oppositional defiant and conduct disorders have worked with children and families from groups of lower social class status who have come to attention of the child protection and criminal justice systems (Rowe & Liddle, 2003). Similarly, the work of Jose Szapocznik has demonstrated how family therapy can be adapted to Hispanic youth and families, with particular emphasis on how to engage families in treatment (Szapocznik & Kurtines, 1989). His work, which has also included therapy with HIV-positive people and their loved ones, has moved the field past the idea that the therapist should wait for the family to be "motivated" enough to engage in treatment; rather, he assumed that wariness of therapy and the chaos that can come with poverty and multiple stressors require that the therapy team make special efforts (extra contacts and phone calls) to induce low-income Hispanic families to get themselves mobilized to engage with an initially alien process of family therapy.

On the other hand, there is practically no research on how family therapy works with immigrant groups from non-Western countries that have no tradition of psychological treatment, such as sub-Saharan Africans and Southeast Asians. The group aspect of family therapy may lend well to people from traditional communal cultures, but there is a great need for more clinical development in this area to accompany work done with previous generations of immigrants (McGoldrick et al., 2005).

A recent promising example of the adaptation of family therapy to non-Western groups comes from Hong Kong, where a team of clinicians and researchers added a family therapy component to their psychoeducational program for childhood asthma. Ng et al. (2008) observed that most asthma psychoeducation programs focus on the illness alone and pay little attention to systemic/familial factors that appear to be so prominent in the families they see. They decided to add a family therapy component and test the efficacy of an expanded approach by looking at both biological outcomes and familial ones. The intervention format consisted of five sessions of asthma management and six sessions for emotional management, with a combination of joint parent–child group sessions, separate child and parent sessions, and joint sessions where parents and children discuss and try out ways of jointly resolving issues related to the theme of the day. The family part was adapted to the Chinese Confucian culture by having a strong emphasis on facilitating self- and mutual appreciation, on showing the mind–body connection, the discussion of traditional Chinese medicine, and the importance of letting the child grow up. Results showed that, in comparison to a wait-list control condition, the intervention benefited the children in the biological markers and adjustment to asthma, and also benefited the parents and the family relationships in most of the relational outcomes. Of note was that the parents felt a greater sense of efficacy in asthma management. The researchers accomplished the task of adapting family therapy to their own culture and demonstrating that it worked as expected in the treatment of asthma in a family context.

CONCLUSION

An important question facing family therapy and all models of psychotherapy is how effective it is in the hands of average practitioners in communities—therapists who are exposed to traditional training programs and then acquire new knowledge and skills as they go through their careers. In other words, how does therapy work when delivered by therapists in community settings, as opposed to therapists trained in specialized models and practicing in university clinics where much of the research occurs. This distinction is often referred to as *effectiveness research* (in community settings with multiproblem patients seen by front-line clinicians) versus *efficacy research* (in tightly controlled research conditions). Family therapy has some initial evidence for effectiveness as seen in a national study of practitioners conducted by Doherty and Simmons (1996). Reports by therapists and patients indicated success rates similar to those found in traditional efficacy studies. But there is a long way to go for family therapy, as for all model of psychotherapy, to determine how well it contributes to the health and well-being of individuals and families who seek help in community settings.

An important and often-overlooked benefit of family therapy is that other family members in addition to the "index patient" might be helped by family interventions. Most therapy outcome studies focus only on the benefits to the person with the identified problem. Involving spouses and children in treatment has the potential benefit of promoting their healing along with that of the person who is carrying the diagnosis. The best evidence for this assertion is in the treatment of alcoholism, where Kelley and Fals-Stewart (2002) document that BCT showed positive gains for children's psychosocial functioning in comparison to individual treatment for the children's fathers. Family therapy, then, may have multiplying effects beyond the benefits for the identified patient.

Family therapy was born in clinical innovation with a grand, global theory derived from cybernetics and general systems theory. Systematic evaluation of its results was not part of the early tradition but has become so now. The movement of empirically oriented psychologists into family therapy in the 1970s and 1980s was a major factor in the development of evidence for its effectiveness. This evidence is not yet on the par with such the "gold standard" evidence-based models such as cognitive–behavioral therapy, but it is increasing every year and expanding to more and more psychosocial and medical problems. The question now is not *whether* family therapy is effective but rather when it is more effective than individual therapy and which populations and age groups benefit most from family therapy.

6

Future Developments

As the usefulness of family systems theory has become apparent, the number of contexts for family therapists has grown. In this chapter, we will discuss some of the cutting-edge areas of work for family therapists—all areas for future development. They include family therapy in schools, with foster care with adoption, in the courts, in prisons, in the military, with genetic conditions, with older adults, in palliative care and hospice, and with community engagement work.

FAMILY THERAPY IN SCHOOLS

For years, too often families and school personnel have been at odds when a child is unable to learn due to learning disabilities or behavior problems. More specifically, the school blames the parents for not motivating or disciplining the child appropriately, and parents blame the school for their child not learning. Recently, more family therapists have begun working in the schools to tackle this problem (Fine, 1995). Some schools have "family

Thanks to the 2008 Marriage and Family Therapy students at the University of Rochester Medical Center for their help in brainstorming this chapter. They are the future of family therapy.

support centers" where teachers, parents, and children can come together to develop a plan to help the child grow educationally and emotionally. For children with significant problems, building this collaborative team is essential to improving their well-being.

For example, Mr. and Mrs. Brown both came from strict families. They did not want to repeat some of the hurt and pressure they felt from their parents' discipline. Because of this history, they vowed to be supportive and openly loving with their children. Their first child, Mary, had a quiet, serious temperament. She flourished at home and at school, having no problem learning to study and make several close friends. Their second child, Tony, was much more outgoing and adventurous. He continually got into trouble at home and at school. He ran into the street as a toddler, scaring his parents. Once in school, he was rough on the playground and had difficulty focusing on his schoolwork. The Browns felt sure that their son would "outgrow his boyish ways," whereas his teachers and counselors at school felt that he needed limits set on his behavior or he was likely to get worse, not better. The school felt that Tony's parents were far too lenient; the parents felt the school had it in for their son.

Parent–school partnerships have become popular in name but are still far from the norm, unfortunately. As with the Browns they can be complicated collaborations to achieve, with a family having one culture and a teacher having another. Focusing on the best interest of the child, something all participants can agree upon, becomes the key to success. The family therapist provides a systemic approach to understand elements of both home and school and create a consistent, safe environment for the child to learn and develop.

FAMILY THERAPY WITH FOSTER CARE

Family therapists have special skills to offer when it comes to controversies about the importance of biology, attachment, and parenting. We have a national crisis about the quality of foster care in the United States; much controversy surrounds the question of when children should be taken away from their parents and placed in foster care and when biological families should be "restored." Studies show that most children do better academically and behaviorally if they have a modicum of contact with their original parents, even if those parents are in prison. Some parents are so impaired or abusive, however, that contact of any kind must be carefully supervised.

Family therapists who have close collaboration with social services organizations can provide assessments and support for biological and foster families. Foster parents deserve parent training and support to manage children in placement who have difficult problems (Fisher, Gunnar, Chamberlain, & Reid, 2000; Nilsen, 2007). Family therapists can act as consultants to peer foster parent support programs. They also can be critical in helping biological parents develop the parenting and life skills necessary to reclaim their children or decide they can no longer raise their child.

FAMILY THERAPY AND ADOPTION

Some people choose adoption because of infertility, others out of a desire to raise children who do not have functional parents. The process of adoption can be stressful. It often involves a bewildering number of choices, including domestic and international adoption, at a time when prospective parents are anxious to move ahead and build their family. A home study is usually required, where prospective parents and their home are evaluated by a social worker. A family therapist can be a valuable support during this process—helping the individual or couple through the decision-making process and helping them to evaluate their own histories and develop parenting skills that may not have been present in their own backgrounds.

In addition to public versus private and domestic versus international, adoptive parents today must also decide about open versus closed adoption. Some select open adoption, wanting their child to know his or her birth parent(s). In these situations, a family therapist can help to negotiate the specific agreement about contact with the child, the birth parent(s), and the adoptive parent(s).

Other adoptive parents do not want to know their child's biological parents, nor do they want an ongoing relationship with them. Some children, as they grow older, are securely attached to their adoptive parents and report they do not wish to know their biological parents. Other children, securely attached or not, become curious during their teenage years or when they themselves have children and begin a search to meet their biological parents. Preparation by a family therapist can be helpful in this emotionally laden situation (Ryan & Madsen, 2007). Biological parents later in life vary in their ability to be welcoming to their offspring. As with children of divorce, some adopted children develop relationships with their biological parents and have families with multiple parents and different kinds of relationships.

FAMILY THERAPY IN THE COURTS

The courts, especially family court, contain many people involved in litigation who have emotional and family problems. Divorce is the most common situation that takes families to court. The key to success for the children of divorce is for their parents to be able to cooperate for the children's sake. Some divorcing couples are so angry with each other that they regularly undermine each other as parents with their children. Supporting their children's homework assignments, for example, can require communication that is rare in couples who decide to separate. Therapists can provide psychoeducational courses for divorcing parents that enhance coparenting skills, focusing both parties on their children's well-being (Pedro-Carroll, Nakhnikian, & Montes, 2001).

Many children go back and forth between their divorced parents' households. Family therapists can help parents find a system that works for their children. These parents may come to family therapy again as the children age and wish to change the visitation policy, for example. This kind of family therapy may occur in consultation with the courts, or it may prevent having to involve the judicial system at all.

FAMILY THERAPY IN PRISONS

There is increasing awareness that many prisoners have partners and children (Bilchik, Seymour, & Kresiher, 2001) and that maintaining these family ties while in prison can foster better community reentry (Hairston, Rollin, & Jo, 2004). A 2008 issue of the journal *Family Process* contained several articles on family therapy and prisons (Imber-Black, 2008). One article reported on an evaluation study on a psychoeducational couples intervention for prisoners (Einhorn et al., 2008). The program improved couple functioning among inmates and their partners. Another promising innovation is sponsored by the Minnesota-based Council on Crime and Justice, working in five prisons with male offenders, their partners, and their children. The intervention consists of a family impact assessment, free transportation for family members to the prison, psychoeducational parenting and relationship groups, and couple therapy for men with partner relationships during and after incarceration. As with other innovative family therapy interventions in nontraditional settings, a major challenge is gaining access and trust with prison officials. The Council on Crime and Justice project has won staff and administrative respect through the results of the psychoeducational parenting groups; men who take these groups have been more cooperative prisoners. Then prison officials were more open to family therapy in the prisons. This work is so new that no outcomes (even anecdotal ones) are yet available, but it holds great promise to meet an important social need. (For information, visit the Council on Crime and Justice Web site at http://www.crimeandjustice.org.)

FAMILY THERAPY IN THE MILITARY

Military families face special challenges, especially during wartime (Kaslow, 1993; Sherman, Zanotti, & Jones, 2005). Mothers and fathers may leave for extended periods of time to serve in countries far from each other and their children. Maintaining a marriage and a connection to growing children requires communication and flexibility. Each time a parent leaves and rejoins a family after a long tour of duty, the couple and the family must reorganize its structure. Family therapists can help couples plan for their separation from each other and their children. Grandparents, other family members, or close friends may move in to help with raising the children. Maintaining the prominence of the parent who is away becomes the duty of all parenting figures. Finding rituals and communication vehicles that support the connection of the child to that parent are important.

Some couples and families are not able to make the transition back to their old status when the family member returns from duty in the armed services. In these situations, family therapists can help facilitate the least destructive separation and divorce, focusing on the children's best interest when children are involved.

For families who lose a member during active duty, family therapists can witness and facilitate the grieving and loss that is so wrenching in these situations. These therapists help the family to find ways to honor the fallen soldier and carry the memory of him or her into the future.

FAMILY THERAPY AND REPRODUCTIVE TECHNOLOGIES

Since the 1980s, reproductive technologies have allowed couples who struggle with infertility the possibility of having a child. With ever-advancing technology, the science is ahead of our understanding of the ethical, psychological, and interpersonal implications of these processes. Medical family therapists are well equipped to work with women, their partners, and health care teams to help with decisions about if and when such technology makes sense for people who often have been trying to have children for years and are desperate to succeed (McDaniel & Speice, 2001).

Most fertility centers in the United States now require couples that use in vitro fertilization with donor sperm or eggs, whether they use known or anonymous donors, to undergo a psychological assessment to ensure they are competent to make this decision, understand and agree on the procedures, and have thought through the many issues involved. The American Society for Reproductive Medicine now recommends that all IVF children be told the story of their conception and have any information about the donors that is available to the parents who raise them. This recommendation is based on reducing the child's sense of genetic ambiguity and the need (especially in the future) for physicians and nurse practitioners to have genetic information to treat their patients optimally. Counseling can be useful for potential parents in reassuring them that they can construct a love story about the child's conception and the great lengths their parents went to in order to have a baby. A nongenetically related parent often needs reassurance before any of these procedures about his or her ability to attach to the child.

For couples who choose known donors, medical family therapists can play a special role in helping the couple define themselves as the functional parent. While the friend or family member donating gametes for the conception will likely be a special person to the child, the gift of gametes must be freely given and the role of the functional parent primary. If these boundaries and roles are not clear before the conception, using known donors is not a good idea.

FAMILY THERAPY WITH GENETIC CONDITIONS

Breaking the genetic code at the turn of this century is revolutionizing the practice of medicine. Understanding the genetic component of chronic illnesses, such as breast cancer or diabetes, allows families who are affected to decide whether or not to be tested for genetic mutations. Medical family therapists can work closely with geneticists and genetic counselors to help family members with decision making and communication about any genetic mutations (Miller, McDaniel, Rolland, & Feetham, 2006). For example, a young psychologist came to family therapy referred by a genetic counselor. Her mother had died of breast cancer, and her mother's sister had survived the same disease. This young woman was ruminating about whether to be tested herself as she approached her wedding date. The family therapist compared her pedigree (a family tree with genetic information) to her genogram and discussed with her the pros and cons of testing at this point in her life. In the end, the young woman decided not to be tested because that it would not affect her management of her health (she would continue close surveillance for breast cancer). Others choose testing and then must decide how to communicate with spouses, children, and other potentially affected family members. Medical family therapy with people with genetic conditions is especially poignant as adult children try to care for parents while watching what may be own futures with illness.

FAMILY THERAPY WITH OLDER ADULTS

When an older adult becomes ill or loses capacity, this situation challenges couples and families to reorganize to care for their loved one (King & Wynne, 2004). If the older adult is the primary caregiver in the family, others must step in and fulfill these roles. For example, women sometimes must adopt the role of financial manager when their husband becomes ill, knowing nothing about the family finances. Or a husband must become the caregiver for his previously independent wife. These changes in role require flexibility on everyone's part, and a consultation with a family therapist is often helpful.

With children, serious illness in their older parents often marks an important point of transition in the roles with their parents, having moved from dependency to autonomy and now to care giving. The roles reverse. Families have varying abilities to make this change smoothly. Family therapy can help to heal old wounds and develop new patterns of communication when needed.

FAMILY THERAPY WITH PALLIATIVE CARE AND HOSPICE

Medical family therapy can be especially useful at the end of life. The decision can be difficult for a patient and family to choose palliative, or comfort, care rather than continuing to intervene and attempt a cure (King & Quill, 2006). This decision making involves communication with the health care team, the patient (if competent), and the family. Sometimes this communication in our fragmented health care system requires significant effort by the family and can be facilitated by a medical family therapist. Threatened loss at the end of life, especially with a dying young person, evokes powerful emotions in families. Medical family therapy during palliative care or hospice can provide a safe holding environment for families to resolve old conflicts and communicate their appreciation and gratitude for each other and their hopes for the next generation.

FAMILY THERAPY AND COMMUNITY ENGAGEMENT WORK

Family therapy began as a movement—not just as another way to do clinical practice. Pioneers like Gregory Bateson and Virginia Satir were interested in larger social issues and wanted to make a difference beyond conventional mental health practice. They saw systems theory as something bigger than family dynamics alone. But this broader vision became difficult to sustain as the field matured, professionalized, and fought for its place in reimbursement systems. There are now a number of promising developments on this front, including Rojano's (2004) model of community family therapy to engage urban, low-income families and Landau's (2007) linking human systems community resilience model, which specializes in work with communities that have undergone rapid transition or traumatic loss.

Another emerging model of community engagement for family therapists and other professionals is the Families and Democracy and Citizen Health Care Project, which draws on family therapy's tradition of interest in larger social issues and adds democratic public theory and community organizing strategies. Doherty and his colleagues have created citizen initiatives on a diverse set of problem areas, including health care (diabetes, depression, smoking); cultural challenges, such as overscheduled children; and family challenges, such as issues facing low-income unmarried fathers (Doherty & Mendenhall, 2006; Doherty, Mendenhall, & Burge, in press). This work stresses the importance of civic engagement to strengthen family life, emphasizes the need to transcend traditional provider/consumer models of health care and professional service delivery, and offers a vision of families and citizen professionals together creating public initiatives. A newly created Citizen Professional Center at the University of Minnesota is serving as training venue for therapists and other professionals to learn this approach to community engagement.

These are just a few of the areas in need of attention by the family therapists of the future. As our society moves from a deficit-based, individual model to a strength-based, relationship model of understanding human behavior, these opportunities will continue to grow, and with them, the need for creative, talented family therapists.

7

Summary

Family therapy was developed in the 1950s and 1960s as a reaction against the psychoanalytic emphasis on the individual. It was also a byproduct of cultural concern about the state of family life, particularly worries about the enmeshed, smothering family that was thought to lead to mental illness. Although psychoanalysis had always concerned itself with early childhood influences, family therapy offered a radical new method to intervene in current family dynamics. It was an American-born approach to psychotherapy and as such embodied Americans' interest in direction, action, and active problem solving.

These pioneers embraced a new theoretical framework that they found outside the mental health world in general systems theory (out of biology) and cybernetics (out of early computer science). Led by Gregory Bateson, the Palo Alto team applied these innovative theories to their analysis of family interactions. Bateson and his colleagues Haley, Weakland, Jackson, Watzlawick, and Satir were particularly struck by the rigid patterns of interaction that families maintained over long periods of time. The Palo Alto team developed brief therapy and strategic family therapy, models that are directive and brief, aiming for rapid change. Jay Haley became the most prominent figure in strategic family therapy.

The other two prominent theoretical models in family therapy's first generation of development were Bowen family therapy and Minuchin's structural family therapy. Working out of Washington, DC, Murray Bowen focused on how family processes foster or diminish the individual's differentiation of self. Combining systems theory and evolutionary theory, Bowen saw individuals as struggling with an evolutionary past that accentuates lower brain functioning and stimulates fight-or-flight anxiety. Anxiety in turn leads to low differentiation of self or the inability to separate the emotional and rational domains of the mind. Anxiety and low differentiation of self are fostered in a nuclear family emotional system characterized by emotional fusion without autonomy, emotional cutoff out of fear of fusion, and conflict through third parties rather than directly (triangulation). Individual forms of psychopathology are the result. The therapist works as a coach to diminish anxiety and promote differentiation of self in the family itself (rather than working to change intrapsychic dynamics related to the family). Bowen's perspective on family of origin issues remains influential today. Tools such as a genogram or time line can be helpful in organizing complex information in simple visual form.

Working in New York City and Philadelphia, Salvador Minuchin and his colleagues developed a structural theory of family functioning and a practical model of structural family therapy. In structural theory, families experience trouble (and children become symptomatic) when their boundaries are too porous (enmeshed) or too rigid (disengaged). The former prevents children from achieving autonomy and the latter prevents them from receiving enough support. These family dynamics are visible to the therapist in the session. The therapist is highly active, like a choreographer or director. The first phase of therapy is joining/accommodating/connecting with each member of the family equally. The second phase is restructuring problematic family patterns through altering perceptions of the problem; through enactments, which are in vivo experiences of an alternative family pattern; and task assignments for the home to stabilize the new patterns. One reason for the prominence and influence of structural family therapy over the past 4 decades has been its straightforward set of practical strategies. Structural family therapy has changed over the years as Minuchin and his collaborators have developed interests in individuals in families and in larger systems.

EVOLUTION OF FAMILY THERAPY AFTER THE FOUNDERS

The second generation of family therapists were rebels like their elders, but now they pushed back against the orthodoxies of family therapy itself. These therapies emphasized a strengths-based approach, amplifying individual and family strengths rather than pathology. The solution-oriented family therapists led by Steve de Shazer rejected theory in favor of brief, focused interventions aimed at capturing the capacity of patients to change on their own, with the therapist as a coach and cheerleader. Like strategic and Bowen therapies, solution-oriented therapy has infiltrated many forms of psychotherapy, although it is infrequently practiced as a pure model of therapy.

Reflecting feminist, multicultural, and postmodern themes in the 1980s, narrative therapists challenged family systems theory as another "totalizing" framework (just like psychoanalysis) created by experts and imposed on ordinary people. Narrative therapists saw people as developing "problem-saturated descriptions" of their lives, which clinicians frequently reinforce through traditional diagnosis and problem-oriented treatment. The goal of therapy is to free people from oppressive stories in their lives, stories derived from the dominant culture (including therapy), which they have learned to describe their problems. The therapist's job is to "deconstruct" this narrative and help the patient reclaim ownership of his or her life. Therapy becomes is a form of conversation that involves "re-storying," in which patients locate and generate alternative narratives that create an altered sense of self that is separate from the problem. The therapist does not diagnose and attempts to not use a substantive theory beyond assumptions about the role of narratives in people's lives. Focusing on cultural scripts, narrative pioneers Michael White and David Epston were explicitly multicultural, profeminist, progay, prolesbian, and opposed to social oppression in all its forms.

The other major developments in family therapy's second generation were radical in a different way: an acceptance of the role of biology and medical illness in a theory and therapy model that had tended to avoid the physical side of human life. Psychoeducational treatment for schizophrenia and medical family therapy reconnected family therapy with its origins in medicine and biology and stressed the importance of collaborative teams from different professions working together instead of the solo therapist or the therapist team managing all of the complexity of family problems.

The third generation of family therapy turned toward integrative approaches focusing on specific problems of childhood such as oppositional defiant disorder, conduct disorder, and substance abuse. These new models were evidence-based from the beginning and combined structural, strategic, and cognitive–behavioral therapy principles and practices into work with families. Inspired by Gerald Patterson's parent training, multisystemic family therapy (Henggeler), multidimensional family therapy (Liddle), and functional family therapy (Alexander) forged elements of the first and second generation models into powerful, scientifically verifiable approaches to difficult disorders of children and youth.

FAMILY THERAPY PROVES EFFECTIVE

Five decades after the origins of family therapy and 3 decades after the first empirical tests of its effectiveness began to emerge, we now know that family therapy is effective for a wide range of behavioral and mental health disorders in childhood and adulthood. Evidence for the greater effectiveness of family therapy over individual therapy appears primarily in family therapy for childhood, adolescent, and young adult problems. These areas include childhood oppositional defiant and conduct disorder, adolescent eating disorders, and schizophrenia among young adults. Among adults, the strongest evidence for unique benefits of family therapy is in behavioral couples treatment for alcoholism among men. As with studies of individual psychotherapy, there is little evidence that one form of family therapy is consistently superior to another.

IDEAS AND TECHNIQUES THAT CUT ACROSS MODELS OF FAMILY THERAPY

In terms of theoretical concepts that cut across models of family therapy, there are four basic, orienting basic questions:

1. How do individuals develop symptoms within families?
2. How do families maintain levels of interpersonal connection that allow for both emotional bonding and individual autonomy?
3. How does family conflict become unmanageable?
4. How can families change dysfunctional patterns?

To answer these and related questions, family therapists developed a number of rich concepts that are defined and exemplified in this book. A central organizing concept is that families can be too close (enmeshed), which leads to lack of autonomy and personal differentiation, or too distant (disengaged), which leads to lack of nurturance and support. In either case, family relationships become strained and family members are apt to become symptomatic or not recover from their medical or psychological problems. As a way to assess this continuum of closeness and distance, family therapists pay a lot of attention to boundaries within families. Boundaries are the way the family defines who is in and out of the family and its subsystems, and how people relate across these subsystems. Family therapists work to clarify confused boundaries, as when a child is treated like an adult sometimes and a child other times, and to strengthen boundaries when they are too porous, as with a parent who confides too much in a child.

Another central conceptual category relates to family organization. Here family therapists pay particular attention to triangles and coalitions, ways that family members align themselves in support of one another and against one another. Family secrets, scapegoating, and conflict via third parties are common examples of underlying triangulation. It is not uncommon for a family member to try to induct the therapist into a coalition against another member; the art is to decline the triangle invitation without alienating the inviter.

A third set of conceptual tools refers to the context of the family. How does the family's current situation reflect multigenerational patterns? For example, how are cutoffs in an earlier generation being played out now? How is the child's oppositional behavior reflecting the long-absent father's role in the family? How are cultural gendered patterns complicating the family's path to recovery? How are poverty and discrimination demoralizing parents who are trying to manage their adolescents? How are interactions with medical, school, and other systems contributing to the problems, and how might these systems be mobilized to help solve problems?

A crucial issue for understanding family therapy in practice is that it is not just a modality for treating relationship problems. Any case can be understood from a family systems perspective, no matter how many people are in the therapist's office for help. Sometimes the referral is for one person, and the family is both collaborator and participant in the treatment. Couples counseling can be effective for people with depression, and we have discussed at length how psychoeducation for families of patients with schizophrenia or bipolar disorder can prevent or reduce relapse rates. Of course, sometimes the referral focuses on a relationship, such as with marital therapy, and in that case the relationship is the "patient." In any case, the therapist elicits the individual, relationship, and social factors that contribute to the continuation of the problem. A good systemic treatment plan focuses on the levels of the system where the therapist, patient, and family can get the most leverage for change.

Another crucial distinction in family therapy treatment is that the relationship between family members is primary, not the relationship between the therapist and the patient or family. In psychoanalysis or psychodynamic psychotherapy, the transference of the patient's introject of a parental figure onto the therapist becomes the grist for interpretation and exploration. In family therapy, it is the *actual* relationships that are the focus of treatment. Behavior therapists may talk with patients about how significant others reward progress or unwittingly reinforce symptoms. In family therapy, those positive and negative reinforcements are available for view directly in the therapy room. Because of this, the greatest intimacy in the room is typically between family members, rather than with the therapist. And the therapist's job is to side with all family members simultaneously, which involves offering balanced levels of support and challenge.

With so much action occurring at once, it is essential that the family therapist be in charge of the process of sessions. Therapist passivity will lead to inaction among low-key families and to runaway sessions among openly conflictual families. The family therapist is a kind of traffic cop—teaching family members to communicate without blame, listen respectfully to each other, acknowledge they heard what was said, and learn to deal with conflict, difference, and emotional intensity. The therapist wants to hear the individual and family stories, to understand their belief systems, and, like an applied anthropologist, to help the family find the solutions to their pain and their problems from within their culture and value systems. The therapist may also be something of a teacher, educating or showing patients how their behavior affects each other.

While family therapy began as a renegade concept, outside of the mainstream of mental health, the acknowledgement of the centrality of family and other close relationships in health has become common. Family therapy is growing. It is now practiced in a variety of contexts from health care to schools and the workplace, prisons, social services agencies, the courts, and the military. In the end, family therapy is about mobilizing the resources of those closest to us to promote healing and restore functioning.

Glossary of Key Terms

ADAPTABILITY Systems theory concept referring to the ability of a system to change in structure or process to meet the demands of a changing environment. Adaptability is a core element in family resilience; even in the face of severe environmental stressors, a highly adaptable family can remain healthy.

BATTLE FOR INITIATIVE As described by Carl Whitaker & Bumberry (1988), the power struggle at the beginning of therapy embedded in the deep desire of the patient to be cured in which the patient acts as if the therapist will "cure" the problem and provide all the "initiative" for that to happen. The therapist must insist that she or he provides the structure for the therapy and the patient/family provide the initiative, or energy for change.

BATTLE FOR STRUCTURE As described by Carl Whitaker & Bumberry (1988), the power struggle at the beginning of therapy embedded in the deep desire of the patient to be cured in which the patient acts as if the therapist will "cure" the problem while the patient controls the "structure" of the therapy, including how the therapist will function, who will attend, when the appointment happens, etc. The therapist must insist that she or he provides the structure for the therapy and the patient/family provide the initiative for change.

BIOPSYCHOSOCIAL APPROACH As described by George Engel (1977), this approach expands the biotechnical model of medicine to include an understanding of the psychological, interpersonal, and community aspects of a health problem. The job of the clinician is to assess these aspects and how they relate to the problem and recommend intervention to the patient and family at the level or levels that can produce the most useful change.

BOUNDARIES   Systems theory concept referring to the interface between subsystems where energy and information are exchanged. Applied to families, boundaries are the way the family defines who is in and out of the family and its subsystems. Boundaries can be clear, diffuse, or rigid.

BRIEF THERAPY   Model developed by the Palo Alto team in which the therapist works quickly and directively to help solve the family's problem, often through strategic interventions such as prescribing the symptom. It represented a break from models that emphasized that understanding the roots of problems was necessary for problem resolution.

CIRCULAR QUESTIONS   As described by Mara Selvini-Palazzoli and colleagues (1980), a tool for both assessment and intervention that involves asking each family member in family therapy to comment on the relationships of other family members. For example, the therapist in a session focused on a child's asthma attacks might ask that child, "What does your mother think about how your father cares for you during an asthma attack?" This process provides rich systemic data and focuses the family's attention on their relationships.

CITIZEN HEALTH CARE   Approach to family and community work in which the therapist and other professionals work democratically with successful patients and other community members to cocreate public initiatives addressing problems in health care and family life (Doherty & Mendenhall, 2006).

COALITION   Negative alliance between two or more family members against another family member. Structural and strategic family therapies, in particular, emphasize the importance of breaking up cross-generational coalitions in which a parent and a child are aligned against the other parent.

COHESION   How emotionally close or distant family members are from one another.

COLLABORATION   Process of partnering, or working together, with patients and other professionals to achieve patient and family goals. Collaboration is a core element in medical family therapy (McDaniel, Hepworth, & Doherty, 1992).

COLLABORATIVE FAMILY HEALTH CARE   Approach to medical care involving close teams of medical and behavioral health providers who work with appreciation of the family's role in health and illness. All team members work from a biopsychosocial/family systems framework that does not divide problems into biological and psychosocial realms but views them as interlocking and thus requiring teamwork among professionals from different disciplines. See the journal *Families, Systems & Health.*

DIFFERENTIATION OF SELF   Bowen's (1978) concept referring to the extent to which a person can separate the emotional and intellectual dimensions of the self and is able to make reflective, autonomous decisions rather than being driven by anxiety.

DISTANCER   As described by Fogarty (1976), "pursuer" and "distancer" are concepts in which any intimate couple unconsciously decides on a comfortable level of intimacy between them. The distancer is the person who is more likely to respond to anxiety by pulling away in a relationship. This movement is likely to invoke pursuing by the partner to maintain the homeostatic level of intimacy in the couple.

DOUBLE BIND   Palo Alto team's concept in which a dependent family member is placed in an impossible situation because of contradictory messages from parents, such as a command to be more independent or to be spontaneously affectionate. The Palo Alto team believed initially that double bind communication was a cause of schizophrenia but later found that it is common in families who do not have a member with schizophrenia.

ENACTMENT   As described by Minuchin (1974), based on work by Ackerman, after assessing the family pattern of relating, the therapist brings about a new pattern of relating in the session itself.

EXPRESSED EMOTION   Concept in family psychoeducation referring to the degree of criticism and overinvolvement of family members toward a family member with mental illness. It is generally measured via a structured interview (the Camberwell Family Interview) in which a parent is asked to talk about the patient's recent psychotic break and hospitalization.

EXTERNALIZING THE PROBLEM   As described by White and Epston (1990), this intervention involves moving the problem out of an individual or relationship and describing it as something external to them. For example, a family may be encouraged to label a chronic illness, such as diabetes or bipolar disorder, as an animal and asked to describe all its features, give it a name, etc. In this way, the family takes charge of the problem, trying to prevent it from organizing an individual or the family.

FAMILY   As defined by McDaniel and colleagues (2005), any group of people related biologically, emotionally, or legally. It is the group of people that the patient defines as significant to his or her well-being, part of the person's natural support system that can enhance health.

FAMILY LIFE CYCLE   As described by Carter and McGoldrick (2005), the epigenetic stages that family relationships move through, from coupling to families with young children, families with adolescents, children leaving home, retirement, families with aging/ill parents, and finally death in the family and bereavement. Building on Erickson's description of the individual life cycle, each stage has its developmental challenges for individual and family relationships. Unresolved problems at one stage are likely to make the challenges of the next stage more difficult.

FAMILY PSYCHOEDUCATION   As described by Anderson (1983), family psychoeducation emphasizes the use in therapy of education about the biology and predictable emotional and interpersonal issues for such problems as schizophrenia, bipolar and other affective disorders, attention deficit disorders, eating disorders, and chronic illnesses such as diabetes or asthma. Family psychoeducation often occurs in multifamily group formats.

FAMILY RITUALS   As described by Roberts and Imber-Black (2003), interventions that support previously developed family celebrations for holidays or other important family experiences, such as a memorial service honoring a loved one. Fiese (2006) emphasizes the importance of family rituals for more routine experiences such as dinnertime or bedtime.

FAMILY STRENGTHS   Concept that underscores the importance of assessing and building on the positive aspects of family functioning to solve the presenting complaint. Focusing on family strengths balances, or offsets, the tendency of clinicians and patients to pathologize their problems.

FAMILY SYSTEMS THEORY   Application of general systems theory from the early 20th century to family relationships. Systems theory emphasizes the relationship between its elements and the fact that the whole is qualitatively different and behaves differently than the sum of individual parts. Family systems theory emphasizes the relationship between an individual's functions (such as a child) and other relationships in the system (such as that between the parents or between the mother and grandmother).

FAMILY THERAPY   Application of family systems theory to psychotherapy; "a psychotherapeutic approach that focuses on altering interactions between a couple, with a nuclear or extended family, or between a family and other interpersonal systems, with the goal of alleviating problems initially presented by individual family members, family subsystems, the family as a whole, or other referral sources" (Wynne, 1988, p. 9).

FUNCTIONAL FAMILY THERAPY   Sexton and Alexander's (2002) evidence-based model that focuses on understanding the functions of the child's disruptive behavior (what he or she is seeking in the family—for example, more closeness); reframing the behavior so that the family take a collaborative, nonblaming set; and intervening through strategic and behavioral approaches.

GENETIC MUTATION   Alteration in the normal DNA structure that can result in congenital anomalies, disease, or higher risk for disease.

GENOGRAM   As described by McGoldrick and colleagues (1999), a figure that organizes family members and family history by generation. It can include dates of birth, marriage, and death; divorces; the quality of family relationships; pregnancies, abortions, and miscarriages; and other information. The genogram is used by most family therapists as a core tool in treatment.

IDENTIFIED PATIENT   Family systems theory assumes that individual problems have relational aspects to them. The "identified patient" is the family member who presents, or is presented, as the main symptom-bearer in the family. For example, a child may present as the identified patient with a behavior problem in school. This problem may signal distress in the parents' marriage; when that distress is alleviated, the child no longer acts out in school.

INDIVIDUATION   Process in which children (and adults) develop individual autonomy in the family. Healthy individuation occurs when the child is emotionally well connected and supported in developmentally appropriate autonomy. It requires clear family boundaries. Family therapists emphasize individuation within relationships and seek to avoid family cutoffs that often lead to pseudo-individuation (a point emphasized by Bowen, 1978).

INTERGENERATIONAL COALITION   Family relationship in which a family member in one generation colludes with a family member in another generation against a third family member. If these coalitions become a pattern, a vulnerable person in the system (such as a child) may develop symptoms. Healthy family functioning is based on strong relationships among members in the same generation and clear communication across generations.

JOINING   Process by which the therapist develops a working alliance with each member of the family. It involves acknowledging family strengths, respecting existing hierarchies and values, supporting generational subsystems, and confirming each individual's feeling of self-worth.

LARGER SYSTEMS   As described by Imber-Black (1988), systems outside the family, such as the community, the workplace, social service agencies, the government, cultural institutions, and a variety of larger entities that have a major impact on the family and individual's functioning within a family.

MAUDSLEY FAMILY TREATMENT   Evidence-based approach to family therapy for eating disorders among adolescents. It is based on structural family therapy in which the parents are put in charge of getting their child to eat appropriately, thus reinforcing the parental subsystem and allowing the child to temporarily rely on parents for self-control. The symptom is "externalized" as an enemy to be combated as a family, rather than blamed on the parents or the child. When the child's weight stabilizes, autonomy is gradually returned to the child (Le Grange, Binford, & Loeb, 2005).

MIRACLE QUESTION   As described by de Shazer (1985) and adapted from Milton Erickson, an intervention that allows the patient and family to envision a successful resolution to their problem. It involves asking a patient or family to imagine that the therapist waves a magic wand so that when they wake up the next morning, their problem is gone. How is life different? How are they behaving? Their spouse? Their children? Other family and friends? Their workplace? Now, what are the first few steps that would be necessary to move toward that goal?

MEDICAL FAMILY THERAPY   As described by McDaniel, Hepworth, and Doherty (1992), an approach to psychotherapy that works to heal the mind–body split. Founded on the biopsychosocial approach and family systems theory, it assumes that every therapy involves an assessment of biopsychosocial functioning—significant health and illness events as well as important intrapsychic, interpersonal, and social experiences. Medical family therapy is a metaframework into which any other kind of psychotherapy can be placed.

MULTIDIMENSIONAL FAMILY THERAPY   Evidence-based approach to treatment of adolescent drug abuse created by Howard Liddle and colleagues (2001) out of structural and strategic family therapy models. It emphasizes building a collaborative alliance with the adolescent as an individual as well as with the parents and community stakeholders.

MULTILATERAL PARTIALITY   As described by Boszormenyi-Nagy and Spark (1973), family therapists strive to form a strong working alliance with each family member, taking sides with each family member so that all experience fairness in the therapeutic relationship; also called "multidirected partiality."

MULTISYSTEMIC THERAPY   Evidence-based, multicomponent model of working with adolescents with behavioral and conduct disorders in which the therapist works intensively in the homes and communities of a small number of families, with the goal of establishing parental control, community support, and rapid return of the child to appropriate behavior. This model uses a wide range of family therapy techniques, including structural and strategic approaches (Henggeler et al., 1998).

NARRATIVE THERAPY   Approach based on postmodernism that emphasizes how problems are created in family and cultural contexts that emphasize pathology. Narrative therapists help people create a new story for their lives and their problems to emphasize their capacity to resist negative cultural images and to take charge of their lives (White & Epston, 1990).

PARENT TRAINING   Evidence-based model of therapy for children with behavioral problems, developed originally by Gerald Patterson (1971) based on social learning theory. The model focuses particularly on coercive control loops whereby the child gains parents' attention primarily when he or she is acting out and helps parents emphasize positive reinforcement, incentive charts, and the use of less aversive and more effective management techniques such as time-out. Parent Training has become more systemic in recent years by focusing beyond the parent–child dyad.

POSITIVE CONNOTATION   As described by Selvini-Palazzoli and colleagues (1980), a family therapy technique in which the therapist puts a positive spin on whatever symptom or issue is discussed by the family. For example, a child's absence from school might be framed as a sacrifice to alert the family that they have not yet sufficiently grieved the death of a grandfather.

PSYCHOEDUCATIONAL TREATMENT   Evidence-based approach to treating schizophrenia and bipolar disorder in which the family is educated about the medical aspects of the disorder and coached on how to maintain positive, low-stress family relationships and engage in low-conflict problem solving and autonomy promotion (Anderson, 1983).

PURSUER   As described by Fogarty in 1976, "pursuer" and "distancer" are part of a concept in which any intimate couple unconsciously decides on a comfortable level of intimacy between them. The pursuer in a couple's relationship is the person who is more likely to respond to anxiety by moving toward their partner and asking for more closeness and attention. This movement is likely to invoke distancing by the partner to maintain the homeostatic level of intimacy in the couple.

RESISTANCE TO CHANGE   As described by Anderson (1983), human beings naturally resist change, however positive that change might be. This fundamental principle allows us to test whether the change is really necessary and desirable. Do I really want to put my energy into changing? Family therapists understand this resistance is inevitable and try to work with (rather than fight) this resistance.

SOLUTION-FOCUSED THERAPY   Approach pioneered by Steve de Shazer (1985) in which the therapist avoids diagnosis and analysis of causes of problems and instead focuses on rapid change via simple change strategies based on the patient's abilities and what has worked for the patient in the past. A classic technique is the *miracle question.*

STRATEGIC FAMILY THERAPY   Developed by Jay Haley (1986) out of the Palo Alto team and influenced by structural family therapy, this approach analyzes how the family is maintaining the problem through efforts to solve it or through developmental impasses. The therapist reframes the problem in terms that suggest the family itself can solve it and works for rapid resolution.

SYSTEMS THEORY   Emphasizes the relationship between elements and the fact that the whole is qualitatively different and behaves differently than the sum of its individual parts. General systems theory swept the sciences such as physics and biology in the early 20th century. In the mid-20th century, systems theory was applied to intimate relationships and families. (See *family systems theory.*)

TIME LINE   As described by Stanton (2004), a tool that, along with the genogram, therapists can use to visually organize family history information. Drawing a time line with a family will often reveal the hidden connections between symptoms and family events such as deaths, marriages, and children leaving home.

TRIANGLES (TRIANGULATION)   Three-party configurations that form the basis for ongoing family interactions. Bowen (1978) emphasized the triangles as emotional configurations with tensions between two people drawing in the third person. Minuchin (1974) and Haley (1976) emphasized the inclusion–exclusion and power dimensions of triangles, such as cross-generational coalitions. In general, a focus on triangles instead of dyads is a hallmark of family systems therapies. A common example in families is a wife with marital problems complaining to her sister instead of talking with her husband.

References

Ackerman, N. W. (1958). *The psychodynamics of family life.* New York: Basic Books.

Anderson, C. M. (1983). A psychoeducational program for families of patients with schizophrenia. In W. R. McFarland (Ed.), *Family therapy in schizophrenia* (pp. 99–116). New York: Guilford Press.

Anderson, C. M., Reiss, D., & Hogarty, G. (1986). *Schizophrenia and the family: A practitioner's guide to psychoeducation and management.* New York: Guilford Press.

Bateson, G. (1958). *Naven* (2nd ed.). Palo Alto, CA: Stanford University Press.

Bateson, G. (1972). *Steps to an ecology of mind.* San Francisco: Chandler Press.

Bateson, G., Jackson, D. D., Haley, J., & Weakland, J. (1956). Toward a theory of schizophrenia. *Behavioral Science, 1,* 251–264.

Bateson, M. C. (1984). *With a daughter's eye: A memoir of Margaret Mead and Gregory Bateson.* New York: Morrow.

Beach, S. (2002). Affective disorders. In D. H. Sprenkle (Ed.), *Effectiveness research in marriage and family therapy.* Alexandria, VA: American Association for Marriage and Family Therapy.

Berg, I. K., & Reuss, N. H. (1998). *Solutions step by step: A substance abuse treatment manual.* New York: Norton.

Berkman, L. F. (2000). Social support, social networks, social cohesion and health. *Social Work in Health Care, 31,* 3–14.

Bilchik, S., Seymour, C., & Kreisher, K. (2001). Parents in prison. *Corrections Today, 63,* 108–122.

Blount, A. (Ed.). (1998) *Integrated primary care.* New York: Norton.

Boscolo, L., Cecchin, G., Hoffman, L., & Penn, P. (1987). *Milan systemic family therapy.* New York: Basic Books.

Boss, P. G. (2001). *Family stress management* (2nd ed.). Newbury Park, CA: Sage.

Boszormenyi-Nagy, I., & Spark, G. (1973). *Invisible loyalties.* New York: Harper & Row.

Bowen, M. (1978). *Family therapy in clinical practice.* New York: Jason Aronson.

Bowlby, J. P. (1949). The study and reduction of group tensions in the family. *Human Relations, 2,* 123–138.

Boyd-Franklin, N. (1989). *Black families in therapy.* New York: Guilford Press.

Broderick, C. B., & Schrader, S. S. (1981). The history of professional marriage and family therapy. In A. S. Gurman & D. P. Kniskern (Eds.), *Handbook of family therapy* (pp. 5–35). New York: Brunner/Mazel.

Campbell, T. L. (2003). The effectiveness of family interventions for physical disorders. *Journal of Marital and Family Therapy, 29,* 263–281.

Carter, E., & McGoldrick, M. (2005). *The expanded family life cycle.* Needham Heights, MA: Allyn & Bacon.

Chamberlain, P., & Reid, J. B. (1998). Comparison of two community alternatives to incarceration for chronic juvenile offenders. *Journal of Consulting and Clinical Psychology, 66,* 624–633.

Christensen, A., & Jacobson, N. S. (1998). *Acceptance and change in couple therapy.* New York: Norton.

Constantine, L. (1986). *Family paradigms.* New York: Guilford Press.

Dattilio, F. M., & Epstein, N. B. (2004). Cognitive behavioral couple and family therapy. In T. L. Sexton, G. R. Weeks, & M. S. Robbins (Eds.), *The family therapy handbook.* New York: Routledge.

de Shazer, S. (1985). *Keys to solutions in brief therapy.* New York: Norton.

Doherty, W. J. (1995). *Soul searching.* New York: Basic Books.

Doherty, W. J. (1999). Postmodernism and family theory. In M.B. Sussman, S. K. Steinmetz, & G. W. Peterson (Eds.), *Handbook of marriage and the family* (2nd ed.). New York: Plenum.

Doherty, W. J., & Baird, M. A. (1983). *Family therapy and family medicine.* New York: Guilford Press.

Doherty, W. J., & Baptiste, D. (1993). Theories emerging from marriage and family therapy. In P. G. Boss, W. J. Doherty, R. LaRossa, S. K. Steinmetz, & W. R. Schumm (Eds.), *Sourcebook of family theories and methods: A contextual approach* (pp. 505–529). New York: Plenum.

Doherty, W. J., & Mendenhall, T. J. (2006). Citizen health care. *Families, Systems & Health, 24,* 251–263.

Doherty, W. J., & Simmons, D. S. (1996). Clinical practice patterns of marriage and family therapists: A national survey of therapists and their patients. *Journal of Marital and Family Therapy, 22*, 9–25.

Duvall, E. M. (1977). *Marriage and family development* (5th ed.). Philadelphia: Lippincott.

Edin, K., & Kefalas, M. (2007). *Promises I can keep: Why poor women put motherhood before marriage.* Berkeley: University of California Press.

Edwards, M., & Steinglass, P. (1995). Family therapy treatment outcomes for alcoholism. *Journal of Marital and Family Therapy, 21*, 475–509.

Einhorn, L., William, T., Stanley, S., Wunderlein, N., Markman, H., & Eason, J. (2008). PREP inside and out: Marriage education for inmates. *Family Process, 47*, 341–356.

Engel, G. L. (1977). The need for a new medical model: A challenge for biomedicine. *Science, 196*, 129–136.

Fine, M. J. (1995). Family-school intervention. R. H. Mikesell, D, D. Lusterman, S. H. McDaniel (Eds.), *Integrating family therapy: Handbook of family psychology and systems theory* (pp. 481–495). Washington, DC: American Psychological Association.

Fiese, B. (2006). *Family Routines and Rituals.* New Haven: CT: Yale University Press.

Fisher, P., Gunnar, M., Chamberlain, P., & Reid, J. (2000). Preventive intervention for maltreated preschool children: Impact on children's behavior, neuroendocrine activity, and foster parent functioning. *Journal of the American Academy of Child and Adolescent Psychiatry, 39*, 1356–1364.

Fogarty, T. (1976). Marital crisis. In P. Guerin (Ed.), *Family therapy: Theory & practice* (pp 325–334). New York: Gardner Press.

Framo, J. (1981). The integration of marital therapy with sessions with family of origin. In A. S. Gurman & D. P. Kniskern (Eds.), *Handbook of family therapy* (pp. 133–158). New York: Brunner/Mazel.

Friedman, E. (1985). *Generation to generation.* New York: Guilford Press.

Gay, P. (2006). *Freud: A life for our time.* New York: Norton.

Goldner, V. (1988). Generation and gender: Normative and covert hierarchies. *Family Process, 17*, 17–31.

Goodrich, T. J., Rampage, C., Ellman, B., & Halstead, K. (1988). *Feminist family therapy: A casebook.* New York: Norton.

Gurman, A. S., &. Kniskern, D. P. (Eds.). (1981). *Handbook of family therapy.* New York: Brunner/Mazel.

Hairston, C. F., Rollin, J., Jo, H. (2004). Family connections during imprisonment and prisoners' community reentry. *Research brief: Children, families, and the criminal justice system* (Winter 2004). Chicago: University of Illinois.

Haley, J. (1976). *Problem-solving therapy*. San Francisco: Jossey-Bass.

Hanna, S. M. (2007). *The practice of family therapy* (4th ed.). Belmont, CA: Thompson Brooks/Cole.

Hardy, K. V. (1989). The theoretical myth of sameness: A critical issue in family therapy training and treatment. *Journal of Psychotherapy and the Family, 6,* 17–33.

Hare-Mustin, R. T. (1986). The problem of gender in family therapy theory. *Family Process, 16,* 15–27.

Henggeler, S. W., Schoenwald, S. K., Borduin, C. M., Rowland, M. D., & Cunningham, P. B. (1998). *Multisystemic treatment of antisocial behavior in children and adolescents*. New York: Guilford Press.

Henggeler, S. W., & Sheidow, A. J. (2002). Conduct disorder and delinquency. In D. H. Sprenkle (Ed.), *Effectiveness research in marriage and family therapy* (pp. 27–51). Alexandria, VA: American Association for Marriage and Family Therapy.

Hill, R. (1970). *Family development in three generations*. Rochester, VT: Schenkman.

Hoffman, E. (1994). *The drive for self: Alfred Adler and the founding of individual psychology*. Reading, MA: Addison-Wesley.

Howard, R. (1981). *A social history of American family sociology, 1865–1940*. Westport, CT: Greenwood Press.

Imber-Black, E. (1988). *Families and larger systems*. New York: Guilford Press.

Imber-Black, E. (2008). Incarceration and family relationships: A call for systemic responses. *Family Process, 47,* 277–279.

Jackson, D. D. (1957). The question of family homeostasis. *Psychiatric Quarterly Supplement, 31,* 79–90.

Jacobson, N. S., & Margolin, G. (1979). *Marital therapy: Strategies based on social learning and behavior exchange principles*. New York: Brunner/Mazel.

Johnson, S. M. (1996). *Creating connection: The practice of emotionally focused marital therapy*. New York: Brunner/Mazel.

Jordin, K. (Ed.). (2003). *Handbook of couple and family assessment*. Hauppauge, NY: Nova Science Publishers.

Kantor, D., & Lehr, W. (1975). *Inside the family: Toward a theory of family process*. New York: Harper & Row.

Kazdin, A. E., & Weisz, J. R. (1998). Identifying and developing empirically supported child and adolescent treatments. *Journal of Consulting and Clinical Psychology, 66,* 19–36.

Kaslow, F. (1993). *The military family in peace and war.* New York: Springer.

Kelley, M. L., & Fals-Stewart, W. (2002). Couples versus individual-based therapy for alcoholism and drug abuse: Effects on children's psychosocial functioning. *Journal of Consulting and Clinical Psychology, 70,* 417–427.

Kerr, M. E., & Bowen, M. (1988). *Family evaluation.* New York: Norton.

King, D., & Quill, T. (2006). Working with families in palliative care: One size does not fit all. *Journal of Palliative Medicine, 9,* 704–715.

King, D., & Wynne, L. C. (2004). The emergence of 'family integrity' in later life. *Family Process, 43,* 7–21.

Lamb, M. E. (Ed.). (2003). *The role of the father in child development* (4th ed.). New York: Wiley.

Landau, J. (2007). Enhancing resilience: Families and communities as agents for change. *Family Process, 46,* 351–365.

Leff, J. P., & Vaughn, C. E. (1981). The role of maintenance therapy and relatives' expressed emotion in relapse of schizophrenia: A two-year follow-up. *British Journal of Psychiatry, 139,* 102–104.

Leff, J. P., & Vaughn, C. E. (1985). *Expressed emotion in families.* New York: Guilford Press.

Le Grange, D., Binford, R., & Loeb, K. (2005). Manualized family-based treatment for anorexia nervosa: A case series. *Journal of the American Academy of Child and Adolescent Psychiatry, 44,* 41–46.

Le Grange, D., & Lock, J. (2007). *Treating bulimia in adolescents: A family-based approach.* New York: Guilford Press.

Liddle, H. A., Dakof, G. A., Parker, K., Diamond, G. S., Barrett, K., & Tejeda, M. (2001). Multidimensional family therapy for adolescent drug abuse: Results of a randomized clinical trial. *American Journal of Drug and Alcohol Abuse, 27,* 651–688.

Lipset, D. (1982). *Gregory Bateson: The legacy of a scientist.* Boston: Beacon Press.

Lock, J., Le Grange, D., Agras, W. S., & Dare, C. (2002). *Treatment manual for anorexia nervosa: A family-based approach.* New York: Guilford Press.

Madanes, C. (1981). *Strategic family therapy.* San Francisco: Jossey-Bass.

Madigan, S., & Epston, D. (1995). From "Spy-chiatric Gaze" to communities of concern: From professional monologue to dialogue. In. S. Friedman (Ed.), *The reflecting team in action: Innovations in clinical practice* (pp. 257–276). New York: Guilford Press.

McDaniel, S. H., Campbell, T. L., Hepworth, J., & Lorenz, A. (2005). *Family-oriented primary care* (2nd ed.). New York: Springer-Verlag.

McDaniel, S. H., Hepworth, J., & Doherty, W. J. (1992). *Medical family therapy.* New York: Guilford.

McDaniel, S. H., & Speice, J. (2001). What family psychology has to offer women's health: The examples of conversion somatization, infertility treatment and genetic testing. *Professional Psychology: Research and Practice, 32,* 44–51.

McFarlane, W. R., Dixon, L., Lukens, E., & Lucksted, A. (2003). Family psychoeducation and schizophrenia: A review of the literature. *Journal of Marital and Family Therapy, 29,* 223–245.

McGoldrick, M., Pearce, J., & Giordano, J. (1982). *Ethnicity in family therapy.* New York: Guilford Press.

McGoldrick, M., Giordano, J., & Garcia-Preto, N. (2005). *Ethnicity and family therapy* (3rd ed.). New York: Guilford Press.

Miklowitz, D., & Goldstein, M. (1997). *Bipolar disorder: A family-focused treatment.* New York: Guilford Press.

Miller, S., McDaniel, S. H., Rolland, J., & Feetham, S. (Eds.). (2006). *Individuals, families, and the new era of genetics: Biopsychosocial perspectives.* New York: Norton Publishers.

Minuchin, S. (1974). *Families and family therapy.* Cambridge, MA: Harvard University Press.

Minuchin, S., Rosman, B. L, & Baker, L. (1978). *Psychosomatic families: Anorexia nervosa in context.* Cambridge, MA: Harvard University Press.

Mittelman, M. S., Ferris, S. H., Shulman, E., Steinberg, G., & Levin, B. (1996). A family intervention to delay nursing home placement of patients with Alzheimer's disease: A randomized controlled trial. *Journal of the American Medical Association, 276,* 1725–1731.

Ng, S. M., Li, A. M., Lou, V., Tso, I. F., Wan, P., & Chan, D. (2008). Incorporating family therapy into asthma group intervention: A randomized waitlist-controlled trial. *Family Process, 47,* 115–130.

Nichols, M. P. (2008). *Family therapy: Concepts and methods* (8th ed.). Boston: Allyn & Bacon.

Northey, W. F., Wells, K. C., Silverman, W. K., & Bailey, C. E. (2002). Childhood behavioral and emotional disorders. In D. H. Sprenkle (Ed.), *Effectiveness research in marriage and family therapy* (pp. 27–51). Alexandria, VA: American Association for Marriage and Family Therapy.

O'Farrell, T. J. (1989). Marital and family therapy in alcoholism treatment. *Journal of Substance Abuse Treatment, 6*, 23–29.

O'Farrell, T. J., & Bayog, R. D. (1986). Antabuse contracts for married alcoholics and their spouses. *Journal of Substance Abuse Treatment, 3*, 1–3.

O'Farrell, T. J., & Fals-Stewart, W. (1999). Treatment models and methods: Family models. In B. S. McCrady & E. E. Epstein (Eds.), *Addictions: A comprehensive guidebook* (pp. 287–305). New York: Oxford University Press.

O'Hanlon, W. H., & Weiner-Davis, M. (2003). *In search of solutions* (2nd ed.). New York: Norton.

Olson, D. H., Russell, C., & Sprenkle, D. (1983). Circumplex model of marital and family systems: IV. Theoretical update. *Family Process, 22*, 69–83.

Panton, J., & Barley, E. A. (2002). Family therapy for asthma in children. *Cochrane Database of Systematic Reviews* (Issue 2). [Wiley Interscience computer software]. The Cochrane Library.

Patterson, C. R. (1971). *Families: Applications of social learning to family life.* Champaign, IL: Research Press.

Pedro-Carroll, J., Nakhnikian, E., & Montes, G. (2001). Assisting children through transition: Helping parents protect their children from the toxic effects of ongoing conflict in the aftermath of divorce. *Family Court Review, 39*, 377–392.

Rea, M. M., Milkowitz, D. J., Tompson, M. C., Goldstein, M. J., Hwang, S., & Mintz, J. (2003). Family-focused treatment versus individual treatment for bipolar disorder: Results from a randomized trial. *Journal of Consulting and Clinical Psychology, 71*, 482–492.

Reusch, J., & Bateson, G. (1951). *Communication: The social matrix of psychiatry.* New York: Norton.

Rigazio-DiGilio, S. A., Ivey, A. E., Kunkler-Peck, K. P., & Grady, L. T. (2005). *Community genograms.* New York: Teachers College Press.

Roberts, J., & Imber-Black, I. (2003). *Rituals in families & family therapy* (Rev. ed.) New York: W. W. Norton & Co. Publishers.

Rojano, R. (2004). The practice of community family therapy. *Family Process, 43*, 59–77.

Rolland, J. (1984). *Families, illness and disability*. New York: Basic Books.

Rowe, C. L., & Liddle, H. A. (2003). Substance abuse. *Journal of Marital and Family Therapy, 29*, 97–120.

Ryan, S. D., & Madesen, M. D. (2007). *International Journal of Play Therapy, 16*, 112–132.

Satir, V. (1988). *The new peoplemaking*. New York: Science and Behavioral Books.

Scharff, D., & Scharff, J. S. (1987). *Object relations family therapy*. New York: Basic Books.

Schwarz, R. C. (1997). *Internal family systems therapy*. New York: Guilford Press.

Sexton, T. L., & Alexander, J. F. (2002). Functional family therapy: An empirically supported, family-based intervention model for at-risk adolescents and their families. In T. Patterson (Ed.), *Comprehensive handbook of psychotherapy. Volume II. Cognitive, behavioral, and functional approaches* (pp. 117–140). New York: John Wiley.

Selvini-Palazzoli, M., Boscolo, L., Cecchin, G., & Prata, G. (1980). Hypothesizing, circularity, neutrality: Three guidelines for the conduct of the session. *Family Process, 19*, 7–19.

Shadish, W. R., & Baldwin, S. A. (2002). Meta-analysis of MFT interventions. In D. H. Sprenkle (Ed.), *Effectiveness research in marriage and family therapy* (pp. 339–370). Alexandria, VA: American Association for Marriage and Family Therapy.

Sherman, M. D., Zanotti, D. K., & Jones, D. E. (2005). Key elements in couples therapy with veterans With combat-related posttraumatic stress disorder. *Professional Psychology: Research and Practice, 36*, 626–633.

Stanton, M. D. (2004). Getting reluctant substance abusers to engage in treatment/self-help: A review of outcomes and clinical options. *Journal of Marital and Family Therapy, 30*, 165–182.

Sullivan, H. S. (1953). *The interpersonal theory of psychiatry*. New York: Aronson.

Szapocznik, J., & Kurtines, W. M. (1989). *Breakthroughs in family therapy with drug abusing and problem youth*. New York: Springer.

Tyler May, E. (1989). *Homeward bound: American families in the cold war era*. New York: Basic Books.

Von Bertalanffy, L. (1976). *General system theory* (2nd ed.). New York: George Braziller.

Walgrave, C., & Tamasese, K. (1993). Some central ideas in the "just therapy" approach. *Australian and New Zealand Journal of Family Therapy, 14*, 1–8.

Watzlawick P., Beavin, J. H., & Jackson, D. D. (1967). *Pragmatics of human communication*. New York: Norton.

Weakland, J., Fisch, R., Watzlawick, P., & Bodin, A. (1974). Brief therapy: Focused problem resolution. *Family Process, 13*, 141–168.

Weihs, K., Fisher, L., & Baird, M. A. (2002). Families, health, and behavior. *Families, Systems & Health, 20,* 7–46.

Whitaker, C., & Bumberry, W. (1988). *Dancing with the family.* New York: Brunner Mazel.

White, M., & Epston, D. (1990). *Narrative means to therapeutic ends.* New York: Norton.

Wynne, L. C. (1983). Family research and family therapy: A reunion? *Journal of Marital and Family Therapy, 9, 113–117.*

Wynne, L. C. (Ed.). (1988). *The state of the art in family therapy research: Controversies and recommendations.* New York: Family Process Press.

Wynne, L. C., McDaniel, S. H., & Weber, T. T. (1986). *Systems consultation: A new perspective for family therapy.* New York: Guilford Press.

Index

About the Authors

William J. Doherty, PhD, is a professor in the Department of Family Social Science and former director of the Marriage and Family Therapy Program at the University of Minnesota. He also directs the Citizen Professional Center. He is author or editor of 15 books, including *Soul Searching* and *Medical Family Therapy* (with Susan McDaniel and Jeri Hepworth). Among his awards is the Significant Contribution to the Field of Marriage and Family Therapy. His current work focuses on community organizing and grassroots democracy in health care and human services.

Susan H. McDaniel, PhD, is the Dr. Laurie Sands Distinguished Professor of Families & Health, the director of the Institute for the Family in the Department of Psychiatry, and the associate chair of the Department of Family Medicine at the University of Rochester Medical Center in Rochester, New York. She is the author of 12 books, among them with Jeri Hepworth and William Doherty, *Medical Family Therapy* and *The Shared Experience of Illness*, and with other coauthors *Primary Care Psychology* and *Individuals, Families, and the New Genetics*. She is a past editor of the journal *Families, Systems & Health*, and currently associate editor of *American Psychologist*. Dr. McDaniel has received many awards, most recently the Cummings/APF Psyche Award for innovations in integrated care.